Reasoning After Revelation

RADICAL

TRADITIONS

THEOLOGY IN A POSTCRITICAL KEY

Series Editors: Stanley M. Hauerwas, Duke University,
and Peter Ochs, University of Virginia

Radical Traditions cuts new lines of inquiry across a confused array of debates concerning the place of theology in modernity and, more generally, the status and role of scriptural faith in contemporary life. Charged with a rejuvenated confidence, spawned in part by the rediscovery of reason as inescapably tradition constituted, a new generation of theologians and religious scholars is returning to scriptural traditions with the hope of retrieving resources long ignored, depreciated, and in many cases ideologically suppressed by modern habits of thought. *Radical Traditions* assembles a promising matrix of strategies, disciplines, and lines of thought that invites Jewish, Christian, and Islamic theologians back to the word, recovering and articulating modes of scriptural reasoning as that which always underlies modernist reasoning and therefore has the capacity—and authority—to correct it.

Far from despairing over modernity's failings, postcritical theologies rediscover resources for renewal and self-correction within the disciplines of academic study themselves. Postcritical theologies open up the possibility of participating once again in the living relationship that binds together God, text, and community of interpretation. *Radical Traditions* thus advocates a "return to the text," which means a commitment to displaying the richness and wisdom of traditions that are at once text based, hermeneutical, and oriented to communal practice.

Books in this series offer the opportunity to speak openly with practitioners of other faiths or even with those who profess no (or limited) faith, both academics and nonacademics, about the ways religious traditions address pivotal issues of the day. Unfettered by foundationalist preoccupations, these books represent a call for new paradigms of reason—a thinking and rationality that is more responsive than originative. By embracing a postcritical posture, they are able to speak unapologetically out of scriptural traditions manifest in the practices of believing communities (Jewish, Christian, and others); articulate those practices through disciplines of philosophic, textual, and cultural criticism; and engage intellectual, social, and political practices that for too long have been insulated from theological evaluation. *Radical Traditions* is radical not only in its confidence in nonapologetic theological speech but also in how the practice of such speech challenges the current social and political arrangements of modernity.

Reasoning After Revelation,

DIALOGUES IN POSTMODERN JEWISH PHILOSOPHY

Steven Kepnes, Peter Ochs,
and Robert Gibbs

with commentaries by

*Yudit Kornberg Greenberg, Susan E. Shapiro,
Elliot R. Wolfson, Almut Sh. Bruckstein,
and Edith Wyschogrod*

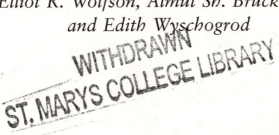

Westview Press
A Member of the Perseus Books Group

Radical Traditions: Theology in a Postcritical Key

Copyright © 1998 by Westview Press, A Member of the Perseus Books Group

Published in 1998 in the United States of America by Westview Press, 5500 Central Avenue, Boulder, Colorado 80301-2877, and in the United Kingdom by Westview Press, 12 Hid's Copse Road, Cumnor Hill, Oxford OX2 9JJ

Library of Congress Cataloging-in-Publication Data
Kepnes, Steven, 1952–
    Reasoning after revelation : dialogues in postmodern Jewish
philosophy / Steven Kepnes, Peter Ochs, and Robert Gibbs.
        p.   cm. — (Radical traditions)
    Includes bibliographical references and index.
    ISBN 0-8133-3506-X (hardcover)
    1. Philosophy, Jewish. 2. Postmodernism—Religious aspects—
Judaism. 3. Judaism—20th century. I. Ochs, Peter, 1950– .
II. Gibbs, Robert, 1958– . III. Title. IV. Series.
B5802.P67K46   1998
181'.06—dc21
                                                            98-20348
                                                            CIP

Contents

PART TWO
Commentary

Introductions

Intellectual Contexts

We offer this book as an introduction to the concerns and voices of a decade-old movement that we have dubbed "postmodern Jewish philosophy." You might well wonder what that phrase means and why we use it. Although we devote much of this book to defining this movement, we are not overly concerned about its name, and we hope you will adopt a similar attitude. For the moment, let us consider the phrase a mere marker indicating the relative position of the movement.

Postmodern Jewish philosophy principally concerns Jewish thinkers who are trained in Western philosophy but who believe that the elemental logics, ethics, metaphysics, and epistemologies of contemporary Judaism can no longer be articulated adequately within the dominant paradigms of modern Western philosophy—that is, the paradigms that link the works of Descartes, Kant, existentialists, phenomenologists, and more recent Anglo-American analysts. In their search for more adequate paradigms, these Jewish thinkers derive support from the work of Continental, academic postmodernists and literary theorists, from Jacques Derrida to Julia Kristeva and Luce Irigaray; but this support is partial, and it becomes effective only when it is reapplied to practices of reading, communal interaction, and social comportment that are irreducibly Jewish. Postmodern Jewish thinkers understand their Jewishness in various ways, but you will see that they share a fidelity to what they call "Torah." Even if they understand "fidelity" and "Torah" in different ways, the differences belong to a community of dialogue, and it is best neither to overstate these differences nor to ignore them. For all, fidelity to Torah means fidelity to communal practices of reading and of social action that have their bases in classical rabbinic interpretations of biblical law and belief, reinterpreted through the generations, and now reinterpreted again in the contemporary, postmodern setting.

One way to practice Jewish philosophy after the demise of the modern Western paradigms of philosophy is to adopt the elemental patterns of Jewish reading and social action as first principles of a Jewish philosophy—refashioning philosophy, one might say, as Judaism writ large. A more modest approach would involve, at a minimum, reforming the principles of modern philosophy so that they are compatible with these patterns of reading and action, reforming philosophy in the manner of Jewish neo-Kantians such as Hermann Cohen. Another way is to frame Jewish philosophy as an open-ended dialogue between contemporary philosophies and contemporary Jewish practices; this often means fashioning models of philosophic practices that are compatible with Judaism, such as hermeneutics, ethics, pragmatism, and semiotics. All of these approaches serve the postmodern Jewish thinker's passion: reintroducing guidelines for moral and religious reasoning into public debates—guidelines that are neither relativistic nor imperialistic but at once definitive and pluralistic, in the manner of classical rabbinic inquiry. All of these ways are examined in this book's discussions of *reasoning after revelation.*

Origins

In 1992, a small group of Jewish thinkers came together in Boston to discuss what we meant by calling ourselves "postmodern Jewish philosophers." In our initial discussion, we discovered that we had overlapping but different stories to tell about the distinguishing characteristics of our Jewish postmodernism. After we parted ways, three of us attempted to clarify our stories—an effort that produced three interrelated but different definitions of postmodern Jewish philosophy. After reading one another's definitions, we came together again to comment on each other's thoughts. After hours of discussion that continued from one day into the next, we concluded that we did have something to say about the meaning of postmodern Jewish philosophy, but that what we had to say was best articulated through a redacted conversation, patterned vaguely after the Talmudic conversations that join together several generations of rabbinic Sages. The Talmudic Sages argued over the meanings of passages in the great collection of rabbinic law and legal philosophy known as the Mishnah, and over the Mishnah's relation to the foundational codes of the written Torah, or Hebrew Scriptures.

In this case, we used a transcript of our brief, initial discussion as a foundational text for our project of self-understanding. We appended our three definitions of Jewish postmodernism to the transcript, treating the definitions as attempts to reduce the transcript's dialogic interplay to some systematic order. Of course, the result was three orders rather than one. We then edited, revised, and redacted the long day's discussion into a series of interactive commentaries on these three orders. Such redaction, we discovered, was not an innocent affair: Even if we relinquished any attempt to reduce our dialogic exchanges to simple theses, we still had to take into consideration the needs of our potential readers. The discussions had to be abbreviated, corrected, and reordered around themes that were recognizable and pertinent to contemporary discussions in the academy. At the same time, we found that nothing could replace the original discussion as the source for these themes as well as for the order and manner in which they should be presented. This is the primary distinguishing mark of postmodern Jewish philosophy itself: Its rule (logos, ratio, torah) cannot be found outside of the dialogic activity through which that rule is enacted.

In addition, if our dialogue were to introduce readers to the emergent discourses of postmodern Jewish philosophy—and not merely to the idiosyncrasies of the three male voices represented in the dialogue—then it would have to be interrupted by other voices in postmodern Jewish philosophy and extended into other precincts of postmodern inquiry. We therefore asked our discussant and four other leading thinkers in the field of postmodern Jewish philosophy to comment on the dialogue as an illustration of major trends in the field. The result is a multileveled gathering of the voices, themes, and styles of contemporary Jewish philosophy.

The book begins with (1) an initial conversation about the meaning of *postmodern Jewish philosophy,* among Robert Gibbs, Yudit Greenberg, Steven Kepnes, and Peter Ochs. We then offer (2) three individual attempts to further clarify the meaning of postmodern Jewish philosophy, by Gibbs, Kepnes, and Ochs. The main text of the book consists of (3) postmodern dialogues—a highly edited, literary rendering of arguments among Gibbs, Kepnes, and Ochs on behalf of their definitions of postmodern Jewish philosophy. These arguments are organized thematically, according to the primary topics of discussion: (a) enlightenment and suffering; (b) *teshuvah* (return) as a distinguishing mark of Jewish postmodernism; (c) Shoah;

(d) suffering, and the Other's freedom; (e) suffering, negative theology, and the face of the Other; and (f) hermeneutics. The book concludes with five detailed commentaries by individual postmodern Jewish thinkers: Yudit Kornberg Greenberg comments on issues of gender and connections to Rosenzweig's thought. Susan E. Shapiro raises questions about the place of the feminine in our dialogue and reexamines Levinas and our post-Holocaust thinking. Next, Elliot Wolfson offers a responsive text-reading of our dialogue with parallels to kabbalistic texts. Almut Sh. Bruckstein develops a responsive philosophic commentary by recalling Hermann Cohen's thought. Lastly, Edith Wyschogrod provides a historical introduction to postmodern Jewish philosophy and a critical extension of central themes of our dialogue. We end with a brief epilogue containing one response to our respondents—that of applying the insights of postmodern Jewish thought to the reading of scriptural texts and developing some new institutions to do this regularly with different communities of scholars, philosophers, and theologians.

The Way We Reason After Revelation

Vayomer moshe el haelohim, Mi anokhi? . . .
Vayomer, ki ehyeh imokh, V'zeh lekha haot
(Exod. 3:11–12)

And Moshe said to God, Who am I? . . .
And He said, I will be with you, and this should be
to you the sign/letter.

When Moses asks the fundamental question of his existence, Who am I, God answers, I will be with you. We returned a number of times to this phrase, *I will be with you,* in our attempts to define what postmodern Jewish philosophy is and who we are as postmodern Jewish philosophers. Postmodern Jewish philosophy is a contemporary attempt to restate the fundamental questions of Jewish existence in a period in which modern philosophy in general and modern Jewish philosophy in particular seem to be at an impasse. This impasse may be perceived as either a point of exhaustion or a point of fulfillment. In the discussions that follow, we explore both possibilities; our attitudes toward modern philosophies and modern Judaisms alternate between these two poles, depending upon the particular issue we discuss. But whether or not we see the failings or the fruits of modernity, we begin with a radical sense of a need to find a new idiom for Jewish thought and life in the present, post-modern period. In our search for a new beginning and in our quest for an answer to the fundamental questions *who am I* and *who are we* as postmodern Jews, we have returned to the Torah and to its theological answer: We are among those who rely upon the promise and who trust that God will be with us. But we do not return to this promise and trust and to God as a concept or an abstract universal. Indeed, one could easily say that religious Jews of all times and places have relied on this fundamental trust and that all forms of modern Judaism are predicated on maintaining continuity with the belief that God is with the Jewish people. What distinguishes us from many modern forms of Judaism is that we have returned to this promise with and through a return to the root texts of Judaism. This is what the great medieval French exegete, Rashi, points to in his interpretation of our opening verse, Exod. 3:11–12. God's promise to be with Moshe is intricately related to the "sign" and "letter" of that trust: the Torah. *I will be with you* means *I will give you the Torah and will be with you through the Torah.* Postmodern Jewish thinking about God, Jews, and the world is not thinking about these entities in abstraction. It is thinking about God, Jews, and the world with the texts of Torah. Here we mean Torah in the traditional sense, as the Hebrew Bible, the Talmuds, and the entire history of biblical and Talmudic exegesis, from the Midrash to the countless Talmudic commentaries. Postmodern Jewish thinking is fundamentally a "thinking with"—with the signs of the Torah about God and the world. It is also a "thinking with" that is not done alone.

Postmodern Jewish thinking is thinking with text and commentaries by a plurality of thinkers. It is not thinking performed by isolated, autonomous, modern individuals in their library cubbyholes but the thinking of Jews with Jews through speech. In Franz Rosenzweig's terms, it is "speech-thinking." In Martin Buber's terms, it is "dialogic thinking." And it is important to see that the dialogue is not only vertical—through the tradition of text and commentary to God—but also "horizontal"—through the living dialogue of Jewish philosopher with Jewish philosopher, in face-to-face conversation. This does not come easily to Western university-trained individuals: It was and is a struggle to think together. Yet we came to see that thinking with each other is rich and complex and exciting thinking. And this is particularly so, as we display at the end of our dialogue, when we think together with the signs and letters of the Torah.

In starting with our particular signs and letters and the language game of Judaism, we have returned home, but we also recognize that we cannot isolate ourselves there. We are modern enough (and we cherish this attribute of our modernism) to appreciate the arts and sciences of modernity, and religions and cultures outside our own. We have received so much training and knowledge from the modern sciences and arts that we could not imagine giving them up. And we have been exposed so deeply to the beauty and the suffering in the world outside our community that we could not imagine turning our backs on it. Our scriptural reasoning—supported by prophetic critique and messianic visions of redemption, and heightened by modern ethics—requires us to be sensitive to victims of poverty, violence, and injustice outside our own communities. This fundamental relationship to the world outside ours means that postmodern Jewish philosophy requires a thinking and acting with and for this outside world.

Thus we come to the Mishnaic and neo-Orthodox expression *torah im derekh eretz*—"Torah with the ways of the world" (*Pirke Avot* 2:2). The meaning we attribute to this phrase differs both from the rabbinic interpretation—that one should have a job in the world to support Torah study—and from Hirsch's neo-Orthodox interpretation—that one should seek to find a harmony between Torah and secular truths. Instead, we seek mutually enriching and critical correlations between Torah and the world. We seek these correlations both in thinking and in acting. Our concern with the world, and our responsive action, is initiated by the meeting of Torah study with modern philosophy and science. Our thinking about the Torah is deepened and made more complex by our knowledge of literary theory, hermeneutics, and semiotics. Our appreciation for ritual is enhanced by our knowledge of sociology and anthropology. Our ethical activities on behalf of others are ruled by the dictates of the prophets and the *halakhah* of *tsedakah* (charity) as well as our understanding of Kantian and Levinasian ethics. Our scriptural reasoning leads us to a critique of the consumerism, narcissism, and disregard for the weak and poor that we find in the contemporary world, at the same time that feminist thought and various forms of ideology critique have led us to look critically at the forms of sexism and abuses of power that are legitimated by and exist within a world ruled by Torah. So *torah im derekh eretz* summarizes the stance toward living and thinking—at times artful and at times awkward—to which we have committed ourselves. It means that as far as we go into the world of tradition and the text of Torah, we do not put aside our university training; and as far as we travel into the non-Jewish world, we bring with us our connections to the Jewish texts that guide and define us.

More than any other thinker, Franz Rosenzweig opened this path to us, in his efforts to correct the faults of modern philosophy and modern theology by a new thinking that focused on language in use. His analysis of the loss of orientation in modern thought prompted a return to traditional texts, but his analysis of them was informed by logical and sociological methods adapted from the university world of his day. If we can, unlike Rosenzweig, remain within the university, it is in large measure due to his development of a non-dogmatic and nonapologetic Jewish thinking.

Philosophical thinking remains vital to our task and to our conversations, and it can be brought into rich dialogue with Jewish traditional texts and religious practices. However, the two cannot be amalgamated; they must retain their distinct identities in the work of postmodern Jewish philosophy. Indeed, there are crucial points of conflict and difference between university philosophy and the thinking arising from the Torah. At these points, each of us as postmodern Jewish philosophers may differ in how we apportion authority between what George Lindbeck would call the cultural-linguistic system of Torah, and the values and principles articulated by a particular philosophical or ethical system outside Torah. The more traditional among us will want to lean toward Torah, and the more liberal among us toward the external system. The more traditional will want to push the borders of the cultural-linguistic system of Torah, text and halakhah, to its limits, the better to meet contemporary values and needs; the more liberal will feel comfortable breaking out of the system of Torah, text and halakhah, to embrace external values.

Whether more traditional or more liberal—and independent of our Orthodox, Conservative, Reform, Reconstructionist, or other denominational tendency—we share a common goal: to forge new and stronger ties not only among Jewish philosophers but also between Jewish philosophers and scholars trained in biblical and Talmudic studies. In the process, we hope to develop ways of practicing Jewish philosophy that highlight our particularities as specifically Jewish thinkers while allowing us to interact with Christian, Islamic, and non-Western philosophers, ethicists, and literary and social theorists who have been brought by the postmodern condition to parallel ways of thinking. We have been greatly influenced by "postliberal" Protestant theologians such as Hans Frei, George Lindbeck, and Stanley Hauerwas, and by Catholic "correlational" theologians such as David Tracy; and we anticipate future productive interchanges with such thinkers and their colleagues and students.

Part One

What Is Postmodern Jewish Philosophy?

In December 1992, Robert Gibbs, Yudit Greenberg, Steven Kepnes, and Peter Ochs met in Boston to discuss what each meant by a phrase we were starting to use in our work: *postmodern Jewish philosophy*. These initial conversations became the basis for the statements, dialogues, and responses collected in this book.

1

Initial Conversation

PARTICIPANTS: *Robert Gibbs, Yudit Greenberg, Steven Kepnes, Peter Ochs*

*   *   *

YUDIT: What defines postmodern thinking and theologizing? How is it different from modern philosophy and theology?

STEVEN: Postmodern thinking is dialogic. It is thinking relationally, thinking with an *and*. It does not follow the Hegelian dialectic, where antithesis nullifies thesis or sublates it in synthesis. Postmodern thinking preserves differences through relation and dialogue. Postmodern thinking is nontotalizing; it seeks no universal, all-encompassing system or story. It is content with particular stories; it celebrates the multiplicity of local stories of truth without trying to reduce them all to the one, the universal.

PETER: I would put it more simply. In order to distinguish the modern from the postmodern, ignore what thinkers claim and look at the logic of the thought. If the logic is dichotomizing, it is modernist; if it is nondichotomizing, it is postmodern.

Y: Elegantly simple, but can't we say more? Postmodernism doesn't exclude in advance; it has no conceptual a priori. It demands neither certain attributes nor their opposites. It seeks the entirety of relationships, the quality of relationships. It is an activity, a process, like the life of an organism. It is a style of thinking.

P: Yes. I see philosophy's essential role as critical, strictly negative. Philosophy is postmodern when its criticism is aimed at repairing. The modern situation needs critique because of suf-

11

fering. Modern philosophy assumes a privileged status without taking note of suffering.

s: Okay. We have outlined some of the characteristics of general or generic postmodernism. But what makes postmodern Jewish philosophy Jewish?

p: Jewishness is crucial. We are not just postmodern philosophers; we are philosophers who are Jewish and philosophers for whom our Jewishness is central to our thinking.

y: What about non-Jews who are writing in this area—writing on Jews and Jewish philosophy and its relation to postmodernity?

p: They are writing about the intellectual part, which is important, but this leaves out the Jewish praxis. Our Jewish praxis defines our particular identity. It defines us not as superior, but as what we are. Non-Jews who do postmodern Jewish philosophy do other things, very important things, but not exactly what we do.

s: So what we are doing here, now, in this little subgroup, is defined partly by the fact that we are Jews who self-consciously affirm their Jewishness and Judaism as central to their thinking. There is a connection between our thinking and our lives, our families, our Jewish communities, and our places of prayer.

y: But our thinking is defined by something more than this fact of being Jewish. We are trying to think in and through the received traditions of Jewish thought toward a particular form and style that we call postmodern Jewish philosophy.

s: And postmodern Jewish theology.

p: But I would start by saying that both theology and philosophy are alien to the Jews. Philosophy entered from the West, from the Greeks—from outside Judaism. Philosophy is the master science, and theology is a subset of philosophy, a subset of metaphysics.

s: But there is an indigenous Jewish theology: it is aggadic, midrashic; it takes the form of narrative and dialogue.

y: But then is it still theology?

s: It depends on your definition of "theology." I apply the term to rabbinic interpretation of Torah and the aggadah or tales we find in the Talmud. This is thinking about God, the Jewish people, and their relation that takes a narrative form. You can call it narrative theology or narrative Jewish philosophy if you want.

Y: But "midrash" and "aggadah" do not capture what we mean by postmodern Jewish philosophy. While we respect these forms of thinking, our thought cannot be reduced to them, because we approach rabbinic thought through postmodern semiotics, hermeneutics, phenomenology, and criticism.

S: Okay. Let's try this. Is postmodern Jewish philosophy like other match-ups between the leading philosophical paradigms and Judaism? In Spain, the paradigm was Aristotelian, and so we had RambaM's [Maimonides's] Aristotelian Jewish thought. In Modern Europe, when Kant was central, we had Jews saying that if Kant wanted a religion, the best one was Judaism. And Jewish thinkers then developed Kantian Jewish thought. Then, when Hegel was the rage, we had Hegelian Jewish thought, then existentialism and Jewish existentialism. And now postmodern thought is central to the academy, and so we have Jews trying to create a postmodern version of Jewish thought? Are we following in this venerable tradition, or are we different? Do we want to say that Judaism is in some fundamental way postmodern?

Were the rabbis actually postmodern, because they thought dialogically and saw seventy faces to each verse of Torah, which means that they anticipated the postmodern's sense of the indeterminacy of meaning? I think that we are doing what Jewish philosophers always have done. We are attempting to match the accepted conceptualization of truth in the general culture with the truths of our Jewish tradition. What do you two think?

Y: Yes, that sounds right.

P: I can accept only one of your two claims: that like our predecessors' Jewish philosophies, our philosophy undoubtedly emerges through a dialogue between Jewish tradition and certain philosophic paradigms of our day—in our case, a postmodern paradigm. But for that very reason I cannot agree that "rabbinic Judaism *is* postmodern." That represents the kind of essentialistic claim we are attributing to modernism: the claim to know what something is. We cannot read our own paradigms into rabbinic Judaism, however much we may discover that rabbinic texts are our best dialogue partners.

S: Fine, I don't want to make it an essentialism, but I think that the rabbis had to respond to a crisis, and they made a way of

living that seems to speak to our postmodern crisis. But to
make the question only one of different kinds of thinking
doesn't quite hold for me. It's too abstract, too contrived, it
leaves something critical out. Let's try this: Let's look at
human lives, the lives of Jewish philosophers. There seems to
be a pattern. These people began their lives in a Jewish environment. They left it for higher education, mastered a science,
and then found that science lacking. Suffering from this lack,
they then returned to Judaism. Look at Hermann Cohen,
Martin Buber, and Franz Rosenzweig: Their lives fit the pattern. Don't we also fit that pattern?

Y: I think that my life fits.

P: And mine and Bob's and most of the others who are part of
our group.

Y: But what is the significance of this?

P: It means that postmodern Jewish philosophy responds to the
anguish of philosophers who don't know where they belong.
We are homeless individuals.

S: Yes, I understand your sense of anguish. You are saying that
it is not just our personal neuroses we are expressing, but that
we are sensing and attempting to respond to something that
many American Jews are feeling and perhaps not articulating.
It is a radical feeling of spiritual homelessness, a sense that the
modern solutions no longer work.

P: Yes, I think we have returned to Judaism as a system of wisdom with world-historical power, its teaching being the power
of human love.

Y: What do you mean?

P: I mean that Judaism is true. Ontologically true.

Y: True, ontologically true!? That doesn't sound postmodern. It
sounds foundational—like a philosophy of presence. The Derrideans would not like it.

P: What Derrideans like isn't necessarily postmodern: It is skepsis, old skepsis in new dress.

S: But do you mean by "truth" an abstract, universal idea?

P: No. I mean something like loyalty, or trust over time, even
love.

S: Not Hellenic Truth?

P: No, of course not. I mean Jewish praxis, Jewish truth that is
not based on the modernist notion of the excluded middle.

s: So you do not mean universal truth but the truth that is particular to Judaism and to living and learning in Judaism?

p: Yes, that is what postmodern Jewish philosophy is about.

y: But if postmodern Jewish philosophy started for us from some experience of pain or homelessness, don't we have to begin with an articulation of this experience?

s: Perhaps we need to begin with a description of some determinative event that launches postmodern Jewish thinking, the way Herzl speaks of his experience of the Dreyfus affair or Fackenheim speaks of the determinative power of the Shoah?

p: I see experience in Charles Peirce's terms as "indexical." Experience has no stuff, no knowledge, no predication. Experience is the sudden here and now. It is interruption; an irresistible force, a demonstrative, a pointing to. Experience says "There!" "Look!" Contentless and indubitable, it requires interpretation.

s: So if we use this notion of experience, couldn't we say that what makes us postmodern is that unlike moderns, we have no single, univocal, decisive "experience" that defines us? We are not burdened by any one defining experience, be it Emancipation, Holocaust, or Zionism. And therefore we don't find compelling the modern philosophies that came out of these experiences: Haskalah, post-Holocaust thought, Zionist thought.

[Robert Gibbs has arrived, and he joins in at this point.]

BOB: Yes, but we not only came after the events of Emancipation, Holocaust, and Zionism; we also see Haskalah, post-Holocaust thought, and Zionism as interpretations of historical events and not revelations of certain truths and foundations for Jewish identities.

p: What I really object to is the dichotomous form of thinking we see in these philosophies: tradition/modernity, Zion/Diaspora, Holocaust/Israel, theism/atheism. These forms of thinking offer either/or choices and attempt to establish universal truths and final solutions for modern Jewish life.

s: And not only did we come after the big events of modern Jewish history but also after the philosophies and ideologies that were created out of these massive events. We live in a time when Zionism, the Holocaust, and Emancipation fail to provide us with a singular basis for our Jewish lives. This is what

I would describe as the predicament of Jewish postmodernity. The philosophies of modern Judaism that were developed in response to certain historical events no longer respond to our current situation. These philosophies have exhausted themselves, and we need to find new ways of envisioning our Jewish traditions and our Jewish lives and new forms of philosophical and theological expression.

Y: So we begin with our experience of pain as an index of something wrong in postmodern Jewish life and thought, and from there we search for a postmodern Jewish form of thinking that "cures" the pain through a search for the truths of Judaism.

B: I think our search will be most fruitful if we take as our model the reading of Jewish texts together. This spontaneous reading-together is a form of Rosenzweig's "speech-thinking" that can help us get to a cross-pollination of social reading and philosophical treatise. Rosenzweig suggests a model of reading where we hear all the voices at the same time. I suggest we try to foster a polyphonic postmodern Jewish philosophy in opposition to standard philosophical treatises, which are monologic.

S: I think you are right that we want to get to the point of reading together. But let's stay with this speaking together for a while, to see if we can bring more clarity to what we mean by the term "postmodern Jewish philosophy."

2

Monologic Definitions

After our initial conversation, three of us—Peter Ochs, Robert Gibbs, and Steven Kepnes—wrote separate definitional statements on postmodern Jewish philosophy.

POSTMODERN DEFINITIONS
PETER OCHS

Since I don't know any privileged way of defining what we mean by "postmodern Jewish philosophy," I will make the topic of "definition" itself an arbitrary starting point. From their Attic beginnings, philosophers have been in the business of referring the many to a one and then telling us as much as they can about that one, even if it meant redistributing it among the many. To speak of the one is in some way to set limits to it, *definere*. *Definition* tends to refer to the job somebody at some place in some time has done to delimit something, usually in the hope of delimiting it fully, at least for then and there. But delimit it by what means, for what purpose, with what consequences?

One characteristic of postmodern Jewish philosophers is that they no longer consider the activity of definition an innocent affair: "You would like us to refer our many to some One?" they might ask. "Well, we wouldn't refuse to do this out of hand" (they are not confident irrationalists or relativists, and they usually like to keep a conversation going), "but we also don't assume that your question is innocent. We do not, for that matter, deny the reality of a One" (they also are not dogmatic deconstructionists), "but we have learned not to identify the oneness of this One with the most general quality of some absolute Being—the quality that Neoplatonic philosophers like Plotinus, for example, attribute to the ultimate goal of their ascent

17

to perfection through some cosmic epoch. We do not dismiss the search for unity, only the presumption of its finality. You might say that we have lost faith in this presumption, since we have seen it lead to so many futile attempts to build Babels, or 'final' systems. We are perhaps also afraid of the presumption, since we have learned, as a horrible lesson of this century, that final systems tend to engender 'final solutions.' "

For postmodern Jewish philosophers, seeking a definition may be like seeking a name in the biblical sense, as exemplified in God's response to Moses in Exodus 3: "'What shall I say your Name is?' ... 'Tell them *I will be with you,* and *I will be what I will be.*'" While God cannot be delimited, God did respond. In Martin Buber's reading, the response is a performative illustration of God's "being there" relationally: The Name is what it is in relation to the one who asks. Human groups like the postmodern Jewish philosophers, of course, have a finitude that keeps them from relating to others so generously; in the image of God, however, they reflect enough of this freedom to be for others to some degree, and thus, to declare to some degree that they will be who they will be in relation to the ones who ask.

But here we are, asking ourselves. For the moment, let us assume that we have posed the question both as a means of drawing ourselves together into a working group and of imagining how to explain ourselves to others who work in the disciplines in which we would otherwise find ourselves: modern philosophy; general philosophy; classical and modern Jewish philosophy, and the history of Jewish philosophy; postmodern philosophy generally; or Jewish theology and postmodern Jewish thought more generally. Here, to declare our name would be first to declare ourselves a group (to offer an index or mark of existence), and second, to display our specific differences from each of these related groups (to limn some identifying characteristics). We have already contributed to the first task by coming together for this discussion. My contribution to the second task will be to suggest what some of our specific differences may be in relation to the other groups.

- *Differences from other Jewish thinkers and theologians.* To start with, our disciplines of inquiry emerge out of dialogue with the Western philosophic tradition, from Plato to Quine. Beyond that, the central problem to which we respond is displayed prototypically in the practice of modern philosophy. This is the problem of modern, typically European, distrust of inherited traditions of knowledge and practice. Richard Bernstein has called this the "Cartesian anxiety": a fear that the ancestral traditions of feudal, Greco-Roman, and biblical society cannot offer first principles for reasoning successfully about a world whose dimensions have been exploded by the industry, exploration, economics, and mathematics of modern civilization. In response to this fear, the Cartesian/modern thinker searches for such first principles in the purportedly autonomous powers of individual human reasoning and imagination. This search is conducted through the vast array of modern inquiries, from historiography to physics, and achieves self-reflective expression in modern philosophy. And we enter Jewish thought in some way molded, influenced, or burdened by modern philosophy.

- *Differences from modern philosophers.* The history of thought and of politics in the past century has given us reason, however, to have as little faith in the Cartesian/modern model of autonomy as the moderns may have in tradition-based knowledge. We therefore join with other postmodern philosophers in criticizing the unwarranted or downright dangerous claims that philosophers make when they overstretch individual lines of reasoning beyond their appropriate spheres.
- *Differences from other postmodern philosophers.* Unlike the more well-known schools of postmodern philosophy, however, our critique of modern system building is not just a more thoroughgoing skepticism, as if we had achieved our postmodernism by overstretching our modern suspiciousness (a rather modern way out of modernity!). To relax Cartesian anxiety, we believe, is to have found again something in which to trust, other than ourselves. Unlike Heideggerian postmodernists, we do not identify this something with the very fact of existence, or with any of its general attributes. Our trust concerns a relationship with the Absolute, but we do not recognize a wholly generic way of reasoning about and describing that relationship. Our way is one that we, as a particular group of thinkers, have inherited as participants in a particular—if variegated—people, with a particular—if variegated—

heritage of linguistic, cultural, and religious practices. These practices are not organized around first principles per se, but around certain primary texts and text traditions—the Tanakh (Hebrew Bible), rabbinic literature, and subsequent streams of interpretations and responses. Our postmodern philosophy emerges as a way of reading these texts, participating in these streams, and thereby identifying, in context-specific ways, the first principles for conducting context-specific tasks of reasoning. These ways of reading and of reasoning display enough generality that we can talk about them with members of other traditions of practice, at times even discovering overlapping principles or blurred borders between one tradition and another. But they are rarely very general, and perhaps never wholly general.

• *Differences from other schools of Jewish philosophy.* Our postmodern readings reconnect us, in some ways, with medieval Jewish philosophy's respect for both biblical/rabbinic hermeneutics and classical philosophy, and in other ways, with modern Jewish philosophy's efforts to refashion the way we mediate the hermeneutical and philosophic traditions. Postmodern Jewish philosophy differs from these antecedents, however, in the modalities it assigns to the words of its primary texts. Unlike medieval and modern philosophers, we are prepared to receive the words as behaviorally and epistemologically authoritative and, at the same time, as vague (or indefinite) and multivalent, and in that sense, as incomplete—that is, as achieving their correct meaning and force only by way of context-specific readings. Rather than placing rationality over and against textuality as a competing or prior practice, we may redescribe rationality as both servant and consort of the text: the activity through which the text both guides our lives and achieves its very definition.

Returning, then, to the topic of definition. The rationality we speak about and seek to perform achieves a different identity among us than it achieved among our medieval and modern forebears. On the model offered in Exodus 3, we may say that this rationality is here-with-us in relation to our needs as specifically postmodern philosophers and that it may be named or defined only as it appears in relation to such needs. It will be what it will be. As the vehicle of our text-readings, it comes to us, furthermore, as the way in which the text will-be-here-with-us. This way may be a manifestation of the attribute of mercy *(midat harachamim)*.

POSTMODERN JEWISH PHILOSOPHY
ROBERT GIBBS

I normally claim that the *post-* in *postmodern* comes from reflection on the destruction of European Jewry. The claim not only reflects the grief and indignation of the community but also points to the utter disintegration of the story of European progress. You can say that Rosenzweig belongs, only because he learned the end of that story from the First World War, but in some ways he is still telling some variant on that all-too-modern story. In place of that story, the Jewish history of the past two thousand years tells us that there has been no appreciable moral or spiritual growth in the wider world. We can even go back another thousand years, because while the Jews may have progressed in their ideas and to some extent in their practices, it would be hard to balance any later generation against that of Jacob, or of Moses and Aaron, or of Solomon. The point quite simply is not that there is no history to be written, but that history does not tell a meaningful, totalizing story (see the work of Walter Benjamin). One cannot take one's bearings from what has happened in history.

Unfortunately, the destruction of European Jewry also marks a turn toward making suffering the key pathos of our thought. It is the intolerable suffering of others that demands our thought, speech, writing, and action. Suffering has pride of place in postmodern Jewish philosophy [hereafter, PJP], more than hope, well-being, or any eudaemonia, more than even knowledge. Suffering pervades our thought and provides a touchstone of reality for all levels of reflection. The first step in our responding to suffering has been an intensification of ethics and responsibility. A smaller circle of Jewish thinkers (Rosenzweig and Levinas, but also Cohen and Buber) has shown a passion to think about responsibility more radically and more honestly in the face of suffering, and in so doing, to protect others from suffering. Whether in face-to-face conversations or in the process of interpreting texts or social institutions, the task of PJP is to make ethics more responsive to the other's suffering and to the other's freedom. Other people, as readers, actors, victims, and thinkers, have their freedom protected by the thinking of PJP. This protection of the other's voice is characteristic of all postmodern thought, but is more accentuated in our context.

The desire to address the general audience, moreover, leads to a most complex conceptual knot. On the one hand, PJP is not exclusively Jewish: It does not in principle exclude any individual or group. It is not analysis of duties, or thoughts, or texts, or practices that only Jews do. On the other hand, it appears in a particularly Jewish context, and it is unwilling to abstract from that context, particularly from the Jewish nature of that context. Thus its particularity must not be seen as dyadically paired with universality—as though if it is Jewish, then it is not universal, and if universal, then not Jewish. PJP can neither maintain a dogmatic attitude (that Jews know or experience or accept some duty or truth uniquely) nor struggle for an apologetic mode that justifies itself solely by the criterion of universality. The criterion of universality must be one merely of possibility (anyone can think this) or similarly of nonexclusivity. The criterion of particularity, moreover, must be maintained firmly: that we think about things this way from our Jewish tradition, in this American context, at this time. But the Jewishness, especially, must be maintained not merely as a point of departure but also as a companion on the road.

But in what is that Jewishness found? Most of all in Jewish books, by which I mean the Bible, Midrash, Talmud, and medieval philosophy and commentary. Levinas makes the argument most emphatically: that Judaism is a potential to be found in the books, even when it is not found in communal practice or thought. To say that Judaism may be found in books is not to see those books as mere containers of information, but to view them as part of a library—as being housed in a series of social practices that create ways of reading those books, and that transmit the books through those ways of reading. The later sedimentation of the tradition reflects the readings of the earlier layers. This Jewish tradition of reading and writing, of texts and libraries, serves as our companion for addressing the suffering of our age, the failure of historical progress, and the freedom of others. For the textual tradition reflects upon parallel sufferings, and offers a logic of interaction and responsibility wherein other people, readers and writers, prophets and scholars, are honored and have their freedom protected. Jewish textuality is at core a way of heeding other voices. Not all voices appear in those texts, and not all of the problems that we face are addressed, but the manner of study and the composition of the text instruct us. To make a companion of these texts is not to make a judgment on the authority of halakhah, or on the fundamentalist question of what was revealed at Mount Sinai, but to become open to a teaching—the Torah.

*   *   *

I wish briefly to take us beyond this inner circle of reflections to show how the three parts of Rosenzweig's *Star of Redemption* can offer an outline of other currents that inform and contribute to PJP. The *Star* used to be read as though it were a book only about language and the experiences of speaking. That reading was partial, reflecting on Part II only, and often not on all of Part II. What I am proposing is that the three parts show us three spheres of inquiry, and that PJP needs each of these spheres in order to perform its tasks. The first part of the *Star* provides a postmodern logic. PJP requires a full set of logical innovations, the cornerstone of which is breaking the models for the relation of particularity and generality. Neither an Aristotelian subordination of species and genus nor a Hegelian totalization of differences into sameness is adequate for PJP. Instead, Jewish particularity needs to be juxtaposed to other particularities, and a logic that can open to generality without dissolving particularity will be the hallmark of PJP logic. Rosenzweig devoted much of his thought to the logic of "and" (parataxis), allowing independent entities to stand in relation with each other without combining to form a third. Even as he explored universality, he maintained the prior independence of the existing person. The role of contingency in his logic of relations is a key to preserving freedom for others.

The central part of the *Star* concerns the hermeneutics of text and speech, and it opens up a range of methods for the study of language. Rosenzweig focuses on what he calls grammar but what we might well term pragmatics, performative dimensions, or grammatology. We can further develop the account of I-Thou conversation and of communal singing, and we also can explore how scientific discourse "knows" the created world. And as I suggested in my book, we can look to the discussion of the scream and of open questions to explore the way that questioning functions in the experience of suffering.

Finally, the third part of the *Star* shows us the need to ground both logic and linguistic theory in social experience. Rosenzweig focuses his sociology on gesture. That focus connects directly with contemporary performance theory and anthropological studies. For Rosenzweig, these social sciences were a way of making ethics true, of implementing the ideals and insights of postmodern hermeneutics. Just as the social sciences can coordinate our ethical relation to suffering, many postmodern innovations in the study of culture and society can help us examine where suffering lies and teach us how to construct institutions that can protect others' freedom. For PJP, this may center around the very same textual tradition—because the legal tradition retains close contact with material culture and with the development of social institutions. The study of Jewish books can go hand in hand with the study of Jewish society, offering reciprocal insight into the ambiguous traditions of the Jewish people.

Postmodern Jewish Thinking

Steven Kepnes

Postmodern Jewish thinking is most lively for me at the conjunction of Jewish subjectivity and Jewish textuality. At this juncture, the modern, autonomous self passes into the postmodern twilight and becomes subject to the play of speech, text, and interpretation; the self-enclosed, rational, liberal, universal self loses its confidence and sets off to find itself in and through dialogue with the textual and human other. The self no longer recognizes itself in itself but through manifold, refracted linguistic forms. Thus postmodern Jewish subjectivity is an interpersonal and communal task requiring constant interaction with Jewish texts. Postmodern Jewish subjectivity involves a "decentering" of the modern, autonomous self through a hermeneutical enterprise of alternately losing and finding that self through the interpretation of Jewish texts. In this hermeneutical and dialogic process, the Jewish self is integrated into the community and the tradition. In decentering the self, this hermeneutical process re-centers Jewish text, or Torah, as the fulcrum around which Jewish existence revolves.

With text/Torah instead of self at center, the primary issues of postmodern Jewish thought become hermeneutical and not psychological. The question is not How do I understand myself, but How do I understand this text. Understanding the text means learning languages—learning about rhetoric, narrative, and metaphor. Understanding Jewish texts means learning about an almost two-thousand-year-old tradition of exegesis. With text/Torah at center, Jewish thought returns to the question of revelation. One cannot put text/Torah at center without facing the issue of its supposed sacredness. How do we understand the text/Torah as sacred text, as word of God? With text/Torah at center, questions of theology come before questions of anthropology. Putting text first does not mean totally abandoning questions of humanity and the human self but seeing the self through relationship to text and to God.

I have used the word "return" a number of times in talking about postmodern Jewish thought, and thus it should be obvious that for me, Jewish postmodernism means a kind of *teshuvah*, a return. For I believe that Jewish modernism at its root involves a turning away from Judaism, a repression of the Jewish for the sake of the modern. One could put this in a number of ways. Modern Jews abandoned their Jewish particularity for the sake of the abstract universal. Modern Jews sought salvation in revolutionary modern ideologies. Modern Jews tried to replace Judaism with ethics and rationality. Or as I often have put it, modern Jews elevated the autonomous self over and above Torah, community, and tradition. Modern Jews seemed to feel that in order to create the new "modern" Jew they had to destroy something of the "old" Jew. All modern Jewish philosophers have their "old" Jews that they despise. Modern Judaism, indeed, was built on the repression, disfigurement, or destruction of what came before. We see this in the Jewish ethicists and existentialists and in the Zionists. Perhaps this is the result of living so long as minorities in anti-Semitic majority cultures—the result of internalizing negative images of the Jew.

Modern Judaism and modern Jewish thought involved a repression and destruction of Judaism; postmodern Judaism is its repair, return, and rehabilitation. This *teshuvah*, as I have said, means a return to Torah, to revelation, to theology; it means a reappreciation, in a myriad ways, of rabbinic Judaism. Yet, the postmodern return to Judaism by Jewish thinkers is not a simple return to premodern rabbinic Judaism. For postmodern Jews do not return to a ghettoized Judaism isolated from other cultures and faiths but to a Judaism set in the context of cultural and religious pluralism. Postmodern Jewish thinkers have grown up and live in a universe where toleration of differing worldviews, if not the actual reality, is presented as an important value of the overarching political system within which we live. Postmodern Jews, however concerned they are to resurrect and rehabilitate Judaism, do so with extremely little desire to denigrate other cultural and religious systems. In this sense, postmodern Jews are like their modern predecessors. Yet, where modern Jews placed themselves in relation to the universal everyman, postmodern Jews stand in a radically pluralized context and place themselves in relation to Christians, Muslims, Hindus, and the countless variety of secularists.

As indicated by the apposition *Torah/text,* postmodern Jews recognize that their Torah stands alongside other "torahs" of the world religions and other texts of world literature. Ludwig Wittgenstein and Clifford Geertz, as well as "cultural-linguistic" theorists of religion like George Lindbeck, have helped us see that every religion creates its own "world" through its own "language-game." Postmodern Jews, Christians, and Hindus are no longer concerned with elevating their language-game to the status of the one true religion. These thinkers are concerned instead with returning to their traditions to relearn the terms and rules of their language-game so that they can play the old, forgotten games once again with friends, parents, and children.

Cultural and linguistic definitions of Judaism present it as a complex symbolic and legal system that is expressed from the outset only through socially and linguistically particular forms. In Peter Berger's words, Judaism is a series of received legitimation and plausibility structures. Judaism is not based on spontaneous insights and personal "religious" experiences. Judaism is not invented anew by every Jew; rather, it is already there, a given, objectivated system that individual Jews need to internalize. Here the paradigm is the internalization of the Passover story whereby every Jew sees him- or herself as going out from slavery to freedom with *b'nei yisroel* (the Children of Israel).

From a cultural-linguistic perspective, a very old doctrine of Judaism abandoned by most modern Jewish philosophers reemerges as a compelling framework within which to understand revelation. This is the doctrine of revelation as *torah she b'khtav* and *torah she b'al peh.* In recalling revelation as the written and oral Torah, I do not want to invoke the fundamentalist notion that the Torah was given to Moshe at Sinai; rather, I want to draw attention to the society-, law-, and text-bound nature of revelation. By invoking the doctrine of revelation as oral and written law, I mean to steer Jewish theology in the postmodern period away from psychological, personal, and mystical terms and toward social, linguistic, and rational terms. This notion of revelation focuses our attention on rituals of initiation and socialization, on education and on strategies of interpretation of the received Torah, which breathe new life into it and make it applicable to the contemporary postmodern situation.

Although I find the cultural-linguistic paradigm most adequate for interpreting Judaism in postmodernity, I recognize that the model is not without drawbacks. First, the model presents a static view of religion and culture. It suggests that the rules and terms, the overarching parameters of the tradition, are set. One's task, then, is essentially a matter of learning the rules and then playing. This model minimizes the extent to which the overarching rules of a tradition— in this case, Judaism—are constantly being negotiated and discussed. In other words, it minimizes the existence of contradiction, dissent, and heterogeneity in Jewish religious ideation and practice. At this point, one would need to introduce historical analyses and enlarge the already important prophetic element of critique in the tradition with the contemporary resources of critical theory. Here we have an array of powerful critical tools offered by Jürgen Habermas, Michel Foucault, and feminist theory.

Secondly, the cultural-linguistic model avoids the question of truth. At some point, as Jewish philosophers, we will want to address the truth-value of our own and other traditions, and the cultural-linguistic model provides no clear guidelines for this analysis. It is essentially descriptive rather than evaluative or normative. Here we will need to employ our philosophical training. I am particularly drawn to the pragmatists and pragmatic theories of truth.

Thus, what I am suggesting is that we need a mixed model for the work of postmodern Jewish philosophy. A cultural-linguistic approach offers us an avenue back to the social, hermeneutical, and ritual traditions of Judaism; and a variety of contemporary theories from pragmatic philosophy will help us to refine, critique, and refashion those traditions in ways that are appropriate to the needs of our postmodern world.

3

Dialogic Practices

Robert Gibbs, Steven Kepnes, and Peter Ochs met again in late spring 1993 to interpret their three definitions of postmodern Jewish philosophy. They attempted to put the dialogic mode of postmodern Jewish philosophy into practice in their discussion of issues raised by the initial conversation and definitions. The resultant dialogues on these issues are reproduced in edited form in this chapter.

Enlightenment and Suffering

Our discussion began with a response to Peter's critique of modernity during our earlier conversation—that "modern philosophy assumes a privileged status without taking note of suffering"—and in his definition of modern thinking as characterized strictly by skepsis.

BOB: It is hard for me to see that the Enlightenment project doesn't take note of suffering. As I see it, one of the characteristics of the Enlightenment project was to oppose Scholasticism for its failure to try to remedy the condition of the world, which means to remedy suffering. The question, of course, is, whose suffering? There is my suffering and there is your suffering. Were the moderns simply not very good at taking account of your suffering, while they were very good on behalf of my own suffering?

PETER: I'd accept that as a helpful distinction. We might say that by identifying with the class of persons who suffered under the oppression of inherited systems of power, Enlightenment thinkers succeeded in defining themselves vicariously as victims, but did not yet see that the victim is another. "Victim" thereby became a universal category of Self (I=I) over and against some heteronomous system, and the response to vic-

29

timization was a categorical imperative to save the self by overthrowing or replacing the system that oppresses it. A postmodern response, in contrast, would take note of the oppressive character of the totalized Self itself, on behalf of its as yet unrecognized Other.

STEVE: If you put it that way, then "postmodern" and "modern" don't sound merely like historically specific periods, but more like recurrent possibilities.

B: You mean that we may have an "eternal return" of "the modern moment" and "the postmodern moment?"

S: Yes. But then it would make sense to add "the traditional moment," too.

P: I like that! Particularly because it would enable us to redefine our postmodernism ordinally, as a position in a series relative to two others. The approach brings to mind Henri Bergson's or Edmund Husserl's or William James's notions of an extended or specious present—some present moment that recalls a past and anticipates a future.

S: So that the postmodern would occupy a place after the modern, which would itself be situated after the traditional.

B: Where "after" isn't a term of chronology, but of logical relation?

S: Or of hermeneutical relation.

P: Each one interpreting the previous. This would mean that some return to "tradition" might tend to follow the "postmodern" moment.

B: But we can't make this scheme too wooden.

S: Let's consider how it works with respect to the issue of suffering. Peter's critique of modernity would seem to cast postmodernism as a critique of the modernist critique of the oppressive character of premodern, or traditional, systems of power.

B: A rather Hegelian scheme.

P: Yes, and it doesn't sound quite right. Perhaps the problem is that Jewish postmodernism isn't settled in its understanding of traditional Judaism. In its critique of modernity, Jewish postmodernism enables contemporary thinkers to reevaluate traditional belief systems, but the character and end of that reevaluation are contested. For starters, there is no such thing as "tradition." Say, for example, we were to identify classical, rabbinic Judaism with "tradition." When we examine rabbinic literature in its Hellenistic environment, we may find ourselves in the middle of conversations not unlike our own, with contests among traditional, modern, and postmodern modes of interpretation. In this case, what would it mean to associate "tradition" merely with "oppressive systems"? That would seem to reflect a strictly modernist way of rereading history.

s: Peter, say more.

p: The modernist approach isolates the oppressive part of some inherited practice, reifies it, and then identifies it with inherited "tradition." The result is that modernists tend to regard their inherited traditions as oppressive overall rather than in some part, and they tend to teach that "a tradition" refers to "someone's oppressive past," from which it is good to be liberated. To avoid imitating the modernist practice, we need to avoid isolating and reifying something that we call "tradition."

s: We need, in other words, to define "tradition" not as a particular place, but as a relational pull within postmodern inquiry: a vector with respect to which the errors of modernity are to be remedied. Through this definition, we would distinguish our postmodern "return" to tradition from neoorthodoxy.

b: Or from counterreformational types of traditionalism, like recent attempts by the Catholic Church to reembrace Thomas.

p: Isn't such neo-Scholasticism a form of postmodernism?

b: No, this is antimodernism; like the 1880s and 1890s romantics, this is an attempt to rediscover a monovalent past. The "postmodern" is absorbed here into either the traditional (as "return" to the true) or the modern (as persistent "criticism" of the true).

s: If you are right, then the neoorthodox may divide history into halves, just as the modernists do. They would disagree only on which half is true—tradition or criticism. To return to what I said before, then, we avoid neoorthodoxy because we do not identify "tradition" with some discrete content but only with a direction within our thinking.

p: What you've said may offer us a way of redefining our scheme: We can bracket any historicist attempt to characterize rabbinic, modern, and contemporary periods of Jewish thought. Instead, we characterize only our own context of inquiry, within which we then valorize three moments. The "postmodern" would represent our way of criticizing our own "modern" criticisms of the traditions of discourse that we maintain. "Tradition" would then represent those collections of texts that bear meaning and require critical inquiry. If those texts were not potentially "oppressive," then we would have no reason to engage in critical inquiry; but if those texts were merely oppressive, then we would *have* nothing worth inquiring about.

S: But wait. Let's get straight what we mean by tradition. We have said it is not a temporal period, and we have said that it is a mode of interpretation, a "vector" with respect to which we criticize the modern, a direction of thinking without specific content. Now, Peter, you say that it is a "collection of texts." I think we need to say that there is a specific content to tradition. Out of the collection of traditional texts comes a mode of thinking, and more than this, a mode of living. I am worried that "tradition" is becoming an abstract, disembodied category for us.

B: And I am not so ready to abandon historically situated claims. Enlightenment thinkers were deeply perplexed that medieval thinkers, as far as they could see, were not trying to ameliorate the human condition. Concern for suffering remains a modern and postmodern concern.

S: Yes, I too do not want to abandon the notion that postmodernity has a contemporary temporal reality. Of course, I accept that it is a mode of thinking with certain epistemological characteristics that we could find in earlier times, but I also recognize that certain cultural, social, and economic transformations are fueling postmodern modes of thinking and calling for a specific response from Jewish philosophers.

P: Why not describe each moment relationally? To describe Jewish modernism this way, we would need to deconstruct any simple identification of "tradition" with all that is premodern. Reform Judaism of the nineteenth and twentieth centuries, for example, offered its modernism as a critique of medieval rabbinic Judaism (of the sixth through the sixteenth centuries), on behalf of what it considered the enduring truths of "biblical Judaism"—among them, the Bible's concern to ameliorate suffering. Whatever the merit of its historical claims, the Reform critique would fit into a relational typology: It criticizes its medieval antecedent for losing touch with the foundational values of its own biblical antecedent. In our terms, Reform Judaism could redescribe what it called medieval Judaism as an inadequate, "modern" critique of "traditional," biblical Judaism. A postmodern Judaism would then, on behalf of "traditional" rabbinic Judaism (first century B.C.E. to sixth century C.E.), redescribe the Reform critique as itself "modern," and so on. In these terms, we might conclude that no Judaism lacks concern for suffering, but that in its concern for a particular type of suffering, each Judaism might forget some other's suffering.

B: That would also imply that each Judaism rediscovers some aspect of "tradition" that another Judaism has overlooked. Thus, we postmodern Jews claim to see something in rabbinic texts that the modern historians of Judaism failed to see, just as those historians made a comparable claim against premodern exegetes.

P: This view would require our redefining our relational typology as a collection of numerous relational pairs, rather than only three. Modern Judaism may describe itself as a critique of medieval, rabbinic Judaism on behalf of some imagined (or reasoned) ideal, but we would redescribe modern Judaism as a critique offered on behalf of some particular but as yet unidentified medieval value. We would then redescribe medieval Judaism as a critique of classical rabbinic Judaism on behalf of certain philosophic or scriptural antecedents. We would then replace the notion of a classical rabbinic Judaism with descriptions of a Talmudic critique of Mishnaic criticisms, a Mishnaic critique of scriptural criticisms, and so on. And we would replace the notion of a scriptural Judaism with descriptions of "intrascriptural" criticisms.

B: This would work only if we defined the whole series of relational pairs strictly with respect to what may be our postmodern preoccupation with suffering and with criticism.

S: Yes, we have something here. But by stressing critique, aren't we moving to a kind of Hegelian thesis/antithesis, a kind of evolutionary dialectic instead of a dialogic model that shows how each form of Judaism was in dialogue not only with the form that preceded it but also with the form before that? A dialogic model stresses the continuities between Judaisms. It

is a form of thinking that in itself provides a method to preserve continuity. The model of critique may work with the
moderns. That, in fact, may be the radical defining characteristic of modern Judaism: cutting off relation through critique.
But the rabbis always presented their innovations through an
interpretive dialogue that preserved continuity with what preceded them. *Pirke Avot* shows this attempt to map out continuity between the Bible and the Mishnah, and I would not call
the *Gemara* a critique of Mishnah but a continuation of its
forms of argumentation and reasoning. We, as postmoderns,
want to capture that modality of interpretive dialogue and
thereby restore the links among the different forms of Judaism.

B: I would distinguish between modern critique and dialogue differently. I think that you are seeing the tradition as too continuous, where the same thing is being repeated, with subtle
variations. I am not sure that dialogue allows for this sort of
continuity. On the other hand, it sounds like you think critique must simply sever relation, must refuse to listen to what
the preceding texts had to say. I would emphasize the discon-
tinuity in dialogue: the way that each interlocutor can disagree
with others, while still listening and learning from them. I
think that if we look at the tradition as a sedimentation of
texts, one on top of the other, we can see that each layer is distinct from what preceded or followed it, and is dependent on
the earlier generations, indeed on the whole set of strata.
Within a scriptural tradition, this means that each stratum of
texts questions the previous one. But in the dialogue of reading, later generations also listen to the earlier generations, or
read them, seeking to be taught, to find something that is currently missing. I would argue this position from the literary
forms of writing: The Mishnaic form is purposely different
from biblical texts; the *Gemara,* especially in the Babylonian
Talmud, engages discussion in a radically different way (more
Scholastic, more digressive, more Biblicist). The links between
generations are not based so much on continuity as on humility: The earlier texts still have something to teach us, something that we don't see at a glance. But the moment of critique
is also real: Those earlier texts also require reinterpretation to
address suffering that has gone unredressed.

P: We could say that postmodern Judaism seeks to delimit the scope of criticism. Criticism is to be offered on behalf of some particular suffering that takes place within an identifiable tradition of discourse, according to rules of criticism that are still to be recovered within that tradition.

B: Provided, once again, we limit this claim to the context of postmodernism.

P: Well, let's try one more redefinition. We began by drawing distinctions between Jewish and generic (or academic) postmodernisms. Can we add that while these postmodernisms may differ in their methods, the corresponding modernisms need not? I mean that Jewish modernism at times differs from the generic or academic sort, but only with respect to the text traditions on which it comments and not with respect to method.

B: We could say that both modernisms attempt to overcome particularity, and both sets of modernists suffer from the consequences of this attempt. The Jewish and Christian Scholastics tended toward modernism in this sense, as did Philo.

S: Yes. And feeling that modern universalisms, from Marxism to ethical monotheism, have failed to bear the utopian fruits they promised, we Jewish postmodernists try to recover a relationship to the particularistic forms of thinking, interpreting, and living that we associate with Jewish tradition.

P: Yes, but to recover a relationship to the particularistic tradition without nullifying modern forms of Judaism.

B: And we do this by maintaining the moderns in our dialogue. We preserve their critique but insist on greater sensitivity to the other person's suffering.

Teshuvah *as a Distinguishing Mark of Jewish Postmodernism*

S: Peter, you wrote that postmodern Jewish philosophy [hereafter, PJP] was organized "around certain primary texts and text traditions—Tanakh, rabbinic literature, and subsequent streams of interpretations and responses. Our postmodern philosophy emerges as a way of reading these texts, participating in these streams, and thereby identifying, in context-specific ways, the first principles for conducting context-specific tasks of reasoning. These ways of reading and of reasoning display enough generality that we can talk about them with members of other traditions of practice." Do you mean that other postmoderns would learn from our interpretations of our traditions' texts, or that they could learn from their own?

P: First, I want to see if we three share a sense of Jewish postmodernism's uniqueness. Perhaps more like the classic Reformers, Jewish postmodernists seem to take a keen interest in looking back to premodern practices of interpretation. Non-Jewish or at least non-biblically based postmodernists do not seem to share this interest. They may, in fact, tend to blame their Hellenic forebears for giving birth to the "modern" project of reducing experience, logocentrically, to single lines of reasoning or single concepts. To criticize this sort of reductionism, however, the Jews don't need to cut themselves off from their past; rabbinic literature itself offers alternatives to, and even polemics against, modern sorts of conceptualisms. The rabbis cannot be faulted for overzealously reducing the many to one; they were masters of polysemic reading.

B: But if Jewish postmodernists can therefore look to their rabbinic forbears for models of nonreductive readings, why can't other postmodernists look to the Neoplatonic allegorists? In their not-Jewish and not-yet-Christian hermeneutics, Proclus and Porphyry, for example, begin to uncover many levels of meaning in the Homeric epics. And Origen's interpretations of the Gospels are explicitly polysemic.

P: With Origen, there are explicit influences from Jewish as well as Hellenistic hermeneutical traditions. As for the others, the most telling mark may be the way the tradition of Homeric interpretation seems to find its fulfillment, after Plotinus, in Christian biblical interpretation. Homeric traditions of multi-layered reading may anticipate aspects of scriptural polysemy, but they don't yet achieve it. They may not, therefore, provide a fully adequate model for the kind of practice that Jewish postmodernists, at any rate, would find satisfying: that is to say, a model for countering conceptual reductionism—or logocentrism.

S: A model, you might say, for "cutting" reductionistic practices? Perhaps we've found a rationale, after all, for maintaining the Jewish rite of circumcision (in some postmodern Jewish circles, you know, the rite seems to be in question): an icon for the Jewish act of delimiting the logos (the phallic logos).

B: Or not just Jewish, but also the generic postmodernism that speaks of castration, if not circumcision—and, at least, of the withdrawal or humbling of the intrusive ego, to leave room for collective dialogue, and for the feminine. Origen castrated himself, you know—and maybe that expressed an excess of logocentrism in his hermeneutics.

P: The phrase "castration, if not circumcision" is troubling; the two terms should be separated as much as "modern and postmodern." The difference between Jewish postmodernists and the others is that the others still believe in the myth of origins. To get rid of modernity they believe you have cut off modernity at the supposed origins of its logocentricity: castrate it. To me, their option is still modern, because in saying a categorical *no* to the phallic logos, they maintain the logic of negation upon which modernity builds its own absolutes. For us, however, circumcision, as opposed to castration, signifies a hermeneutic that preserves the text—or tradition or impulse—while delimiting its potential oppressiveness.

S: So modernism means a practice of cutting off what troubles you rather than reforming it (circumcising it).

B: Whereas the Jewish virtue of repentance, or *teshuvah,* is not to cut off some offending practice, but to reform it by referring it back to something within the depths of that practice that will guide its reform. And if modernism excludes something like the Jewish practice of *teshuvah,* then it leaves only those two options: Become part of a nomological covenant and accept the limitations it imposes, or else cut yourself off from it altogether.

P: Origen, and Philo too, may have operated in environments that offered hermeneutical options like these: Either accept the literal sense of the scriptural text or cut it off (if it offends you). In response, they developed allegorical options: suggesting that, if the literal sense is inadequate, then make it show another layer of meaning. But they lacked a way to delimit this other layer, without reducing it either to what functions as another literal sense or to what we understand simply through our own subjectivity. So what we get at this point in Origen and Philo is a hermeneutic of simple meaning plus indefinitely expanding allegorical meanings, without any nonreductive way of delimiting this expansion. They offer only two options: the route of hermeneutical relativism or that of foundationalism. The first option is to say that the text opens itself to an infinite array of possible readings, each specific to one convention or another. The second option is to say that at least with respect to a potential reader's place in the path of life, these readings may be ordered according to a hierarchy of allegories. Perhaps we should call this option a relaxed foundationalism, since neither Philo nor Origen are rigidly dogmatic about the hierarchy one must adopt; they merely have strong perceptions of it. Philo's strongest perception, for example, is of a path of readings that corresponds to the soul's path of spiritual clarification through disembodiment. We should not assume that this kind of spiritualization is simply irrelevant to rabbinic hermeneutics. The notion of a hierarchy of readings suggests that the text displays its meaning with respect to where one is on one's path of life: There are stages of life to which God's corrections can and cannot be revealed. But correction is not the end of the matter. Rabbinic hermeneutics is not reducible to mere radical deconstruction, because the rabbinic readers' "circumcised hearts" allow them to cut away certain illusions, and through the clearer path that remains, to perceive certain things positively.

B: I am glad you have cited the prophets, and Deuteronomy, where the heart becomes circumcised. The prophetic call for a moral/spiritual turning reminds us that underlying what you are calling rabbinic "hermeneutics" is rabbinic ethics: The rabbinic reader's task is repentance, *teshuvah*. For postmodernists, this means turning back to traditions of practice from which modernity has cut itself off. Citing the prophets' words may also remind us that the prophets used the image of "circumcision" as a trope for a moral/spiritual activity.

S: But not only as a trope, in every case. Let's not spiritualize the prophets' understanding of cult or law, nor, for that matter, the rabbis' understanding.

B: No, I don't mean to do that. I am trying to bring up my concern that with our talk of circumcision and castration, we are just jumping on a bandwagon occupied only by men in the contemporary conversation. That's why I want to say that we are using these terms as tropes, right?

s: Yes.

B: Well, then those tropes may have served their purpose, because we seem to be in the process of replacing them with more accurate and literal terms.

s: You mean, in our talk of "repentance"?

P: Or, couldn't we say, of "reform," as opposed to replacement or excision? We could describe postmodernism as a way of reforming modernism rather than replacing it with something altogether new.

B: That is like Vico's argument against Descartes and Cartesian method in 1700. Vico objected that scientific method required the study of history, particularly the history of rhetoric, and that it was impossible to arrive at truth by abandoning all of the past. He was shocked that they thought a nonhistorical study of math and logic would yield truth in human matters. Vico therefore devoted himself to historical research, even though he regarded himself as a Baconian and a thoroughly modern scientist. We might need a different way of reviving and analyzing the philological disciplines, but we cannot do without them: This is what humans do—they make cultures, laws, languages, and literature.

s: In different terms, the Oedipal model of reform is not adequate: I mean constructing and seeking to overthrow an offending tradition or practice as if it were the oedipal father. The alternate, postmodern model is one of dialogic reintegration with the father.

B: The father as re-membered. Repentance for both father and son (son, in this case). This introduces the possibility of a different way of doing history: the study of history as a form of repentance. Through such study, we re-member a past whose sins are also our sins. The only alternative is to accept them—confess them, as Rosenzweig says—and then reform them, or repent.

P: We appear, then, to have collected two marks that distinguish a Jewish postmodernism from the generic sort. One mark is the stress on maintaining continuity with modernity; the other is acknowledging our own sins. A Jewish postmodernism may want to distance itself from the starkly antimodern righteousness of other postmodernisms. Jewish postmodernism as *teshuvah*—reforming modernity, not abandoning it.

Holocaust

S: Bob, in your statement, you claimed that "the destruction of European Jewry also marks the turn to making suffering the key pathos of our thought," but in the conversation in Boston you agreed with my position that we postmoderns have no one "experience" or event that defines us. We are not burdened by any one historical experience, be it Emancipation, Holocaust, or Zionism. What do we want to say about our relationship to the Holocaust and suffering?

B: If we claim to take suffering more seriously, we cannot avoid addressing the issue of the suffering of Jews in the Holocaust and the place of the Holocaust in postmodern Jewish philosophical discourse.

S: I agree that the Holocaust is a marker for us. It is one of the important markers of the end or failure of modernity. It is one of the modern events we come after, an event that we are "post." I would not use the term "post-Holocaust" to define us, however. That term is too associated with post-Holocaust theologians like Richard Rubenstein, Emil Fackenheim, and Irving Greenberg, who present the Holocaust as an orienting or epoch-making event and allow the Holocaust thereby to shape and determine the central questions of Jewish theology.

P: Yes. I also do not find the term "post-Holocaust" helpful in defining us. I recognize that the term is very important in the popular imagination and is important for situating postmodernity historically. But it does not help to mark the philosophical moves we are trying to make.

S: As we said in Boston, the event of the Holocaust does not generate the terms of our discourse. The Holocaust marks an end, and after it we are trying to begin anew. We do not want to begin with the Holocaust agenda—with the issues of theodicy or anthropodicy, with an absent God or with the world's abandonment of the Jews, or with the Nazis and their war against the Jews.

B: When I say that we are post-Holocaust, I do not mean that we come after the Holocaust to pick up the pieces, to save the remnant and to figure out the implications for theology. I mean we come after the discourse established by the Holocaust.

P: But here I want to say *again* that for me, "postmodern" is not historical. It is a recurring phase, a way of thinking, that can be found in many historical periods. Postmodernity did not need the Holocaust to occur. Postmodern thinking occurred a century before the Shoah. The differences between different ways of thinking are not adequately reflected in the differences between historical epochs. There may be some complementarity between thought and history, I am not arguing against that. But the complementarity is very general and inexact.

S: But here I disagree. I do not think that Jewish thought can be divorced from history. One of the main points of the narratives in the Torah is to show that Jews must take account of their history. What happens matters for Jewish people's thinking about themselves, the world, and God. Isn't that the point of God's action in Egypt, in the Exodus, and at Sinai? God comes to reveal his presence and his will in history. Don't the prophets constantly point to history as the theater of Jewish sin and redemption? Doesn't the rabbinic attention to the details of living life in the concrete historical situation mean that history matters? Doesn't the whole tradition of *Responsa* mean that rabbinic thought is constantly responding to the issues of contemporary and historical Jewish existence?

B: If we are going to put ethics at the center of our discussions and if we are going to address the suffering of victims, then it seems to me that we are talking in the shadow of the Shoah. If Jewish thinkers are going to begin with suffering, how can they avoid the Shoah? The Shoah brings us to the reality of suffering of victims with the greatest vividness and starkness.

S: But when we talk about the logic of postmodern thinking and we talk about getting beyond the Western individualistic self, when we talk about other themes in postmodern philosophy, then the Holocaust is not central. That is why I say that the Holocaust is one of the issues we need to address but it is not the one focal issue.

P: But I think it would be an insensitive reading of nineteenth- and early twentieth-century history to wait for the Holocaust to address suffering. We are already in the belly of suffering in the nineteenth century and we already have antecedent human slaughters and genocides.

s: Like the Russian pogroms against the Jews in 1881 and the Armenian genocide of 1915?

p: Yes, those are just a few examples. But my point is, I am a Jew, but I do not learn about suffering by reading only about my own people's suffering. This is one tendency of Holocaust theology that is troubling to me. Beyond that, I fear that the evil of the Holocaust may have clouded our ability to think meaningfully about other evil: as if before the absolute suffering of these Jews in this event, we cannot speak at all meaningfully about other suffering or others' suffering except in relation to it. In the Israeli context, Adi Ophir has put it this way:

> The presence of evil in Nazi Germany is so intensive, decisive, and so near in time and place, that it appears to threaten to erode any attempt to examine the concept of evil in its modern historical context. On the contrary: The evil that Nazism embodies is apprehended both as a threat and as evident, so much so that it serves as an absolute, objective criterion for judging other forms of evil in other contexts. [from "Beyond Good/Evil: An Outline for a Political Theory of Evils"].

s: We may say, then, that after the Shoah there is a rethinking of modern Judaism that is part of the rethinking I associate with postmodern Jewish thinking. "After the Shoah" is a way of saying "after the failed solutions of modern Judaism." We are after the happy philosophies of Judaism that married the Jewish notion of Providence with modern progress and the modern salvific ideologies of socialism and democratic capitalism. "After the Shoah," or "post-Holocaust," is one of the markers of the new beginning that is postmodern Jewish thinking.

Suffering, and the Other's Freedom

p: Bob, in your definition you claimed that the response of PJP is to intensify ethics. You wrote that "the task of PJP is to make ethics more responsive to the other's suffering and to the other's freedom."

b: That seems obvious from our earlier conversation.

p: Not altogether. It is clear that we are concerned with the other when we move from suffering to our response. That movement clearly has to do with intensifying ethics and responsibility. You would say that the concern is the positive side of philosophy. But how do you infer the idea of others' freedom? And why do you use this phrase that other people "have their freedom protected" by the thinking of PJP? I don't know what that means.

B: It means that our own work is a series of deconstructions. That our own programs have to be made vulnerable to critique so that our thought does not claim a sort of compelling, impregnable perspective.

S: But how does that protect them?

B: It protects them from our thinking, from us. Not only is what they think or how they've suffered at risk, but even their freedom to act is at issue. A theory, a set of laws or commandments, a canon of authoritative texts can be used to disempower people, too. In one sense, liberating another is really about safeguarding their freedom.

S: Why will they need protection? Why are we so mean?

B: Because thinking or talking or acting in any way runs the risk of controlling and assimilating others, of rationalizing their suffering. We need some move to check ourselves.

P: I can imagine what a feminist would say here—that this is a male concern, to look at postmodernism as self-limitation, only because the male ego in modernity has been allowed to overgrow. Where is empowerment, she might ask. What does postmodern Jewish thinking mean for someone who has been in the position of the victim? Postmodernity is not a new way to delimit our own discursive freedom but a chance finally to speak. In Aviva Cantor's words, "the Jewish community must enfranchise women," not limit their power.

S: Well, that's fine, but I would say that some postmodern feminists are saying that getting power is not the goal, that reversing the poles isn't enough. That getting power for themselves to speak without protecting other people's freedom and agency won't do them any good.

P: Just as long as we don't try to tell them what to say.

B: But some of the French feminists do say that reversing the poles is not enough. It cannot be one sort of prophecy, where we tell others that they should not be content with merely grabbing power. But it can be another sort of prophecy, where we announce our own extreme responsibilities and say that

limiting our own power to protect others is what we're trying
to do.

s: But this is straight Levinas, isn't it? You remind me of Levinas's claim that the ethical obligation to the other is dispro-
portionate, asymmetrical—in the language of the rabbis, that
the other's material needs are my spiritual needs.

b: Well, my point is *related* to Levinas. It's only someone who
wants a day in the sun who thinks that the main thing is to
have a chance to talk. It is important for me to have a chance
to talk, but it's more important, ultimately, that other people
have a chance to talk.

p: I still have some problem with the word "freedom." What are
you calling this other person's freedom that you are protecting? I don't know why you don't just use "the other," or "the
other's being," or "the person," "the life," or "the soul." Why
freedom?

b: Because the intellectual violence that we've perpetrated on
them is not merely limiting what they are but also what they
can will. This is Rosenzweig, also Levinas.

p: But do we need to buy into a late modernist language that is
so egocentric that it thinks of the person as an individual will?
This is just a relic of the substantive self. You seem to want to
protect the substantive self. I think about other needs than
freedom, because the other is not an autonomous monad.

b: No, I don't mean to make others autonomous, because we cannot do that, but to protect their independence from my force.

p: But independence is a monadic consideration. I wouldn't want
to keep the others independent. Independence is a state of
loneliness.

b: I don't think it has to be lonely. Look, the argument goes
something like this: In the modern project, the goal was for
me not to be oppressed. It was to get myself liberated so I
could be free and independent. That's the modern project, and
the thing that I most feared was that anybody would make a
claim on me that I didn't want. The solution was to say that
nobody gets to make a claim on anyone else that that one
doesn't want. That was democratizing equalization. Nobody
has any privileges. As I take it, the postmodern project is not
saying "no privileges." It's saying that the other has privileges
but I don't. It's not that now I should protect myself from his

oppression. It's that I now should protect him from oppression. Levinas has an essay called "The Rights of the Other Man," and another essay called "The Humanism of the Other Man." I am indeed receiving that modernist construction of a self but in a new context, a context where the asymmetry of my relations with others privileges those others. That construction of a self gets a function completely different from what it had in the modernist discourse. There is something very important about being willing to die to protect another person's rights for independence, for freedom.

P: This is a case where we need a nondichotomizing logic. It is not "either you're free or I am free." My own freedom doesn't have to be limited in order for you to be free.

B: But there's no discussion of my freedom here. I'm not "free" at all. It's not a zero-sum game—only that my words need to respond to the other person's needs.

S: You just used this asymmetry again, but you're presupposing it without having established the legitimacy or the meaning of that asymmetry. I think Levinas's asymmetry is an odd construct, even though it comes from Jewish sources. For the reader who doesn't know the material, it doesn't follow self-evidently from the phenomenology of suffering. It needs to be worked up a bit so that the notion of asymmetry itself is made more apparent. That's very important. It is a particular path that could be taken from suffering, but not the self-evident path.

P: This is one of the examples where Levinas and Rosenzweig hook too much into the dichotomous options of modern thought.

B: I think the argument is that the only way to protect the other from suffering is to distrust myself radically. If you look at it as trying equally to prevent each of us from suffering, then I, as the one who thinks or controls or judges, will always give my own concerns first place. A reciprocal concern about suffering is too contaminated by my own strategic interests.

P: But if you reconceptualize the whole thing and stop making individual rights the goal, and if you see in the Jewish community that the goal is a series of dialogic relationships around the table, then maybe you won't need to follow Levinas in reversing Hegel and overstating the authority of the other. Perhaps the answer is to throw out that logic of sub-

stantive selves with their independent wills. The entire, Continental predicament of ego and other, even turned around, just
doesn't help us.

B: My position is that you can't throw it out. You have to invert
it. We take the illusion of control and autonomy, and we turn
it inside out. We cannot pretend that we don't think in the aftermath of a modern world that sought to make each individual independent and sovereign, but we can take that desire to
protect me and turn it around into a desire to protect the other
person.

S: But what happens to the community, then? The whole problem with independence is the fracturing of social relations.
Maybe that is why modern Judaism is so hard on Jewish
community. If you struggle to make the other people independent, aren't you still going to shatter community?

B: Inverting the desire for rights, or for independence, or whatever, is not the goal. I wouldn't stop with inverting modern
subjectivity. Rather, the goal is certainly a companionship with
others that is not asymmetrical, but the entry to that companionship is an asymmetrical duty. What binds us to each
other is that each is liable for the other—and that is a way of
seeing the responsibility to protect the other's integrity.

P: What you have just said is helpful, because it contextualizes
what otherwise appears an unnecessarily extreme position.
Levinas's demand for asymmetrical duty is meaningful once it
is restated *with respect to*, and in the terms of, modernity's
egocentric project; presented independently of that project, it
appears hyperbolic and therefore misleading.

B: What about my last sentence in that paragraph? Do you find
protection of the other's voice as irritating as the protection of
their suffering and their freedom?

P: No, the voice belongs more to our discourse, provided you
make clear to whom it is speaking, specifically.

Suffering, Negative Theology,
and the Face of the Other

P: In your statement, Bob, you say that "suffering has pride of
place in postmodern Jewish philosophy, moreso than hope,
well-being, or any eudaemonia, moreso even than knowl-

edge." Does this mean that for Jewish postmodernism, revelation presents a negative face? Does revelation show itself by
way of suffering, as the interruption of some human activity?
So that revelation says "no" to some ongoing activity?

B: I would want to say that God's revelation to us is an interruption, and that interruption alerts us to a suffering we have
been ignoring.[1]

S: Is revelation the correct word here? Isn't revelation tied up
with the Torah given by God at Sinai? I would be more comfortable with another term, another way of putting it. You
said, "suffering has pride of place" for our thinking.

B: But the wake-up call that alerts us to suffering also commands
us to remedy the suffering. We are alerted not only in order
to know but also to act. I want to call this "revelation," because it teaches us (like Torah) and commands us. But the
focus on suffering is, I think, an important characteristic for
our reading of Torah.

P: If we are going to associate Jewish postmodernism with a concern about suffering, we could divide up the moments in our
typology this way. Modern criticism provides marks—indexical signs in Peirce's sense—of the oppressive character of some
aspect of traditional discourse. A particular community is
made aware of some instance of suffering through these
marks.

S: Why call those marks revelation? Aren't they opposed to the
traditional revelation?

B: I think the moderns should not be seen as simply freethinkers
or secularists. They are like one-dimensional prophets: They see
only what is oppressing them in the tradition. But while they
cannot retrieve anything positive from the tradition, they are
finding suffering that has gone unnoticed. Justice does move
them, and if we see them only as indicating where something is
not good enough, then we still are learning from them.

P: This attention to suffering appears in traditional rabbinic discourse, too. The rabbinic tradition of commentary and reflection on the Torah models this reading as alerting us to suffering. One essential element of that tradition is to depict
revelation as God's coming to offer assistance to the one who—
or the people who—suffers. This is how Michael Fishbane cites
the midrash *Exodus Rabbah* (30:24) on Isaiah 56:1:

"Thus said the Lord: Observe what is right and do what is just; for soon My salvation shall come" *(ki qeroba yeshu'ati lavo)*. [The homilist] begins with a philologist's observation: "Scripture does not say 'your salvation' (second person plural) but 'My salvation.'" And he adds: "May His name be blessed! For were it not [so] written [in Scripture], one could not say it." . . . [the derashah continues] "If you [Israel] do not have merit, I shall perform [the salvation] for My own sake *(bishvili)*; for *kivyakhol* [as it were], as long as you are in trouble, I am with you, as it says [in Scripture]: "I am with him (Israel) in trouble" *(imo anokhi be-tzarah)* (Ps. 91:15).

Thus, God is with Israel in suffering, which means that God is with Israel sufferingly!? "That is," says Fishbane, "in shared pathos."[2]

We could say that for the modernist, God shares pathos by delivering the sufferer from oppressive systems of discourse. According to the postmodernist, the modernist's complaint is a reliable sign that something has gone wrong, but it fails to tell us precisely what and where the problem was and is. It is in that sense a doubly negative revelation: It negates something, and it fails to provide positive information about what that something is. That information comes only when the sign is reread in dialogue with the rabbinic tradition's own rules for interpreting such signs. The modernist is not in a position to enter into this dialogue and is therefore not in a position to receive positive revelation.

s: Peter, I have a number of questions here. First of all, it seems that we are not talking about revelation but about salvation or redemption. God's response to suffering is to save people from it. This may also be revelatory, revealing God's saving power, but again I would want to preserve the term revelation for something else. The Torah uses the symbol of the burning bush, or *ehyeh asher ehyeh* (I will be present as I will be present), or the revelation of God's will or word at Sinai. What is revelation to you?

p: When we're at Sinai, we see the clap and hear the thunder, but nothing else. The content comes later.

s: Isn't this positive revelation, revelation of God's presence? How does it relate to the revelations of human suffering?

b: Revelation is a two-party relation, requiring interpretation by the human who receives it. The core is the interruption of my world, the breaking in upon me, that alerts me to others' suffering, others' needs. Whether this is commissioning me to go lead my people from Egypt or giving me ten commandments. Revelation is not information about God, but a shock that requires me to interpret the sign that the shock is.

P: So modernity's complaints are merely negative revelations, but postmodernity's corrections are a way of rereading those revelations in the light of traditional discourse?

B: Like Rosenzweig's distinction between *Gesetz* and *Gebot:* the commandment interrupts, the law stabilizes.[3] The commandment is not complete without the act of interpretation, but in itself it requires only human affirmation.

S: Buber may be interpreted as saying something like this—that the Torah's revelations are direct and positive but content-less: We are not commanded to act in a certain way but instead are commanded something, which we hear as our being told to act in a certain way.

P: Buber would fit in, provided our hearing is constrained by the God we do not otherwise see.

S: Buber may, indeed, provide for less constraint than you may want. In *I and Thou,* Buber seems to say that all I-Thou meetings offer a glimpse of the eternal Thou, which is a minuscule revelation of God.

B: And Levinas might give us a better model for the constraint. The face of the other person is as constraining as your model of revelation, but it has no content.[4]

P: And this refers to the face of God?

B: No. It's a human face.

P: And how do you separate them?

S: Doesn't he claim that it's the image of God?

B: Absolutely not. There's only one passage where he even dares to compare them, but he denies that it is the face of God. And later, he makes the face itself enigmatic.

P: And the face of God isn't enigmatic?

B: Yes, but—

S: And the face is infinite. So there is a relationship.

B: The relationship is profoundly passive. What Levinas says is that in the experience of the face, God has passed by. There's no presence, only a trace.

P: But that is enough.

B: Enough, but only for this model of revelation. Because this model is a negative one, negative contextually. The context is modernity's broken relationship with traditional texts. Derrida also writes in this context, but he also applies his model beyond it. You cannot claim that all positive revelation is impossible, if your negative claim is made against finite traditions or communities. But we can respond to deconstruction on two levels. The first is to describe modernity as the context for the negative revelation—as the context for a deconstruction theologically understood. This is the No to the idols, the foundations, the absolutes, and the essences that modernity tried to establish. That No points from the failures of modernity toward an infinite other. On the second level, however, we can explore contexts other than this modern one, contexts where the infinite might admit of positive characterizations. This is a movement from a Schellingian negative philosophy to a positive one.

S: In their experiences of interrupted and discontinuous discourse, postmodern philosophers in general may share the conditions for negative philosophy. That may account for Levinas's general appeal. The face of the other is a negative revelation. Postmoderns can allow that much revelation to slip in.[5]

P: Perhaps the positive can slip in for Jewish postmodernism in the dress of the negative, by way of postmodern readings of the classic sources. For example, the biblical narrative can be read as a history of Israel's periodic destructions, in relation to each of which Israel comes to some level of self-understanding. Out of its misery, Israel calls on God for both explanation and help, and receives back laws through which it may renew its life, but as a transformed people. Illustrations are the Exodus; enslavement in Egypt; and the Deuteronomic cycles of heroic leadership, failure, and prayer. Can't we see here faces of God as destroyer? Not only destroyer, of course, but one whose rod, in Isaiah's terms, is an indexical sign of the failures of a given level of Israel's political-religious organization.

S: But how is God Israel's destroyer in the Exodus story?

P: God comes as Israel's savior only after the Egyptian oppressors have relieved Israel of its familial, or patriarchal, level of organization. While the story portrays God as one who hears the cries of Israel, it also portrays a divine plan in which God sends them off to their fate in the first place.

s: But you are offering only a partial reading. You are presenting a view of God as destructive, without also noting God's redemption and creation.

p: No, this is only to situate creation—as re-creation—in the context of some destruction. God is the one who tests the limits of a given language system, deconstructs it (a kind of destruction), and allows it to rebuild itself, a new order.

s: It is the rebuilding that the Derrideans won't allow, isn't it?

p: Because they know only the modern context of interrupted discourses. But Jewish postmodernists retain their "traditional" texts as contexts for rebuilding traditional discourses rather than merely deconstructing them. The advantage of Jewish (and in this sense, also of Christian) postmodernism is that its texts provide a prototype of the infinite author of deconstruction as well as of the creator. Outside of Scripture, I don't believe postmodernists have any prototype for the agency of infinite deconstruction. I don't know any Hellenic source for this infinity, either.

s: For the rabbis, Hashem is the merciful one, *middat harachamim* (the attribute of mercy).

p: And Elohim is the one who judges, *middat hadin* (the attribute of justice). But the destroyer may be stronger than this: For the God who destroys inadequate systems of discourse can no longer be known by way of those systems.

b: The inscrutable attributes of this God express, from the human side, the inexpressibility of the loss in these destructions. This is definitely the God you want to stand in a relationship to when you are recovering from a catastrophe or mourning or in grief—the God you want to rail against like Jeremiah—as in Jeremiah's vision of a God who destroys disproportionately: The Jews take one false step, and he wipes them out. It is a very powerful expression of the soul to be in relationship to that kind of God. This is what it means to be grappling with excessive loss.

p: Have you, then, offered a reading of the turning point, when God the destroyer becomes the redeemer? If in a moment of total loss the Israelite looks and asks what is the ground of this loss and finds no answer within the extant vocabulary, because the answer surpasses any language of suffering, then, without a word to explain the suffering, the Israelite is launched into the infinite-as-destroyer—infinite because it is beyond all words. But the moment the Israelite then turns to that destroyer and asks in anger, Why did you do this, then the turning becomes prayer. At that moment, the destroyer is on the way to becoming a redeemer.

B: The listening infinite.

P: Only the infinite can heal, if there is to be any healing, but only when the infinite itself is destroyed. That is God's attribute of mercy, to give up the infinite—to give up the only attribute modernity comprehends in God! As infinite, the infinite will always also be a destroyer, since the finite is deconstructed with respect to it. Giving up its infinity, the infinite can heal, by allowing the systems it has destroyed to transform themselves in ways that permit healing.

S: I am perplexed by this. The infinite one appears to be both destroyer and redeemer.

P: For the order of knowing; I know this one first as destroyer, and only then am I able to recognize that only the infinite can redeem, if it will redeem. It is a transforming recognition, which also transforms the modern into the postmodern—transforming the conditions for negative, infinite revelation into conditions for possibly positive, embodied revelation.

S: Isn't that Job's vision out of the whirlwind: God as destroyer, creator of leviathan?

B: Or consider the Talmud's claims that after the Destruction of the Temple an iron curtain descended, or that all gates are closed except the gate of tears. Why should the gate of tears still be open? And what does it mean that it is open, if not precisely that access is now through the grief itself? It is a doorway to the destroyer.

P: Powerfully said! You have articulated a logic of redemption: One cries for the infinite, and if the infinite does hear, then we have a transformation from the negative theology of interruption to some positive speech. For our modernist colleagues, the narrative stops at the point of referring destruction or deconstruction to the infinite. It has to stop there for them, because once one starts to say that the infinite redeems, then the redeeming has to take some concrete form, and that means a positive form, beyond the limits of negative philosophy. Isn't

that where the trouble comes for the modernist—with con-
cretion and the pleasure that accompanies it?

B: Pleasure?

P: Well, in the sense of the pleasure of redemption. Do you find
that the infinite that commands ever redeems as well? Is there
a point at which the No has ceased and has become the source
of some particular Yes?

B: I think the point is, in part, that the command of the No is
not contingent on there being a subsequent Yes.

P: Good enough. The No comes first.

B: And it comes first with no guarantees, so it cannot be instru-
mentalized—because the only way to get to a Yes is to go
through a No?

P: Good.

B: But there can be a Yes! also. I mean, just as the child can cry in
the night, the child can smile at you also. You work to relieve
the suffering, not on the condition that they will do something
nice in return, but also not without the hope that they will do
something nice. There is a lot of hope without an expectation.

P: Good! But we also cannot reduce the Yeses to hope. Hope belongs to negative philosophy: It's its limit case, or asymptote,
as Norbert Samuelson would say. But the Yes represents one
step more, the beginning of positive philosophy, or theology.

S: But if you take that step, won't you have to give up generality? Negative philosophy has the infinite, after all, but positive
philosophy would seem to give it up in exchange for the concrete moment.

P: So the Yes has no phenomenology?

S: Not a generic one—only a language-specific phenomenology.

P: Are there any other generic characteristics of the Yes that we
can talk about?

S: Perhaps only the narrative of suffering. The narrative form is
generic, but the story of suffering is specific, language specific.

P: Is the testimony of our pain the Yes, or is that the hope—that
by bringing our dead up to God's altar, we bring the story of
our suffering up as well, as if to say, Okay, I know it's your
fault, you have destroyed us; look at what you've done? We
would not waste time doing that unless we had some hope. So
the narrative of our suffering belongs to hope, not to the Yes.

S: But we posit the narrative. Why wouldn't it belong to the Yes?

B: Because it offers no answer to our suffering. The Yes is going to be an answer.

S: In that case, the Yes would be messianic.

B: No, it interrupts messianism.

P: The messianic is hope; it says "there will be one day." But we are talking about now. That is why we have the Talmud to study here and now. The Yes is now.

S: The taste is now. The Talmud is a taste of the world to come, but it is not the world to come. Shabbat is a taste.

B: I would say that the other who commands you, for whom you offer your service, can respond to that offer with friendship. But this response is not the completion of redemption by any stretch of the imagination. That doesn't mean that it is not re- demptive or that there isn't a certain kind of fullness in that response. It just isn't infinite. It is the finite Yes.

P: Okay, then, to return to the description of narrative. If we de- scribe narrative as the story of suffering that we bring, with hope, to God's altar, we have described what may be the emo- tional center of our lives. But that remains a center of hope, of waiting. We have yet to describe what it is like, concretely, to receive some immediate answer. The love song that God would sing for us—a Song of Songs—would not be a narra- tive, because the narrative is what we tell, with hope. The song would represent some other form of discourse that we have not yet described. What would it sound like?

S: Jewish kids laughing.

P: On the streets of Jerusalem, a wedding song?

S: Rosenzweig talks about choral singing, singing the *Hallel,* the psalms of praise, in the synagogue. Thus the form of discourse we are looking for may be a new melody for the *Hallel* or for the *Kedushah* in the *Amidah* that everybody suddenly knows, and everybody sings a different part of the harmony.

*   *   *

B: . . . I am still sad. I find it devastating that for all these cen- turies, philosophy has devoted so little of its resources to con- soling and to relieving suffering. Philosophy was definitely ob- sessed with the pain and the struggle of change and death, but it was so selfish. I just can't understand why there aren't books and books and books, and whole schools of thought, devoted to these kinds of questions.

P: Philosophy was a divine consolation, and life was suffering? But we are talking about pragmatic philosophy, which is a kind of medicine for curing pain, not a consolation.

B: But I am also thinking about exiles and genocides and war. Look, as late as Hegel, you can get a great philosopher justifying the continuing presence and practice of war as not merely a necessary evil—that there should be war—but as an inherent part of the logic of life.

P: So that there was not enough hope available for these philosophers to invest philosophy in pragmatic, redemptive activity, as opposed to a consolational activity?

B: I don't know. I feel that perhaps they were like guards who deserted their posts. I don't know that we're going to make that much difference, you know. But it seems so obvious that we have no choice but to try.

S: This just sounds too melancholic. Where is the joy of study and of practice?

P: Steve, if you are asking about the essence of rabbinic Judaism, then, indeed, the texts of Judaism are studied in joy, not melancholy. But I believe that we turn to a narrative of suffering for strictly epistemological reasons. We are not interested in talking only about suffering: We don't only suffer. But now, after modernity, we know that we cannot prove anything universally except that wherever anyone claims there is suffering—wherever we see someone in pain—suffering is there. Marks of suffering, therefore, enable us to begin conversations across community borders—not to complete them, but to begin. Within our community, of course, we can make claims on the basis of joy or about joy, but only within the community.

B: Well, you can try, but I certainly don't know whether it will work. That is why joy doesn't drive me in the same way. I'm not sure communities have such a strong agreement and peaceful relations within themselves. That is why I resisted your understanding of pleasure.

P: You used two terms. One was hope, one was work. Sad hope, or work, and one engages in the work, you say, without knowing whether or not it will work. To work agnostically in this way would be to work again out of hope! Hope alone would not supply me with the energy that is needed to work in this postmodern project. So I have to work out of faith rather than hope, and that means in response to gifts received directly from an Other, rather than in response to promises. Receiving these gifts is the pleasure I spoke of earlier. Hope is not sufficiently pleasurable.

S: Peter, you seem to be pointing to the limits of philosophy. Like Rosenzweig, you are suggesting that philosophy only takes us so far and then theology takes over. Rosenzweig tells us in the opening of the *Star* that philosophy cannot deal with death and suffering; it attempts to take away the sting but fails, and at this point, theology must come to respond.

B: But Levinas takes up the task—as philosopher—and devotes much of his analysis to suffering, to fatigue, labor, persecution, and so on. I think that Rosenzweig wrote of the limits of philosophy in a modern cast but that postmodern philosophy is well equipped to go beyond those limits.

P: I would hope that our conversation now takes place beyond those limits and allows for a way of speaking that is philosophical and theological at the same time.

S: But Peter, Levinas himself retains a difference between doing philosophy and the theological interpretation of texts, when he describes Western philosophy as the temptation of temptation, the insatiable desire that tastes without risking. Isn't that just what you described as hope without faith?

B: I guess that I hope that postmodern Jewish philosophy can overcome that thoroughly modern idea of philosophy by turning to Jewish texts. The two sides interpenetrate more fully. And there is pleasure. Remember that child I spoke of, crying in the night. There's a great deal of pleasure to receive from the child—an inordinate amount of pleasure in the child's response, in her friendship and love. But she represents the kind of demand one makes of you that can be filled—unlike the demands made on philosophers by the sight of those whose suffering they cannot relieve. They can hope, at best. But you can provide for your child here and now. Two kinds of faces, you might say: one whose demands are infinite, and one finite. The one stimulates negative philosophy—as well as hope and sadness. The other warms you with love and the pleasure of giving.

P: We can also speak of a third face, then: one that offers infinite love. I am puzzled by this face, of course, since from what
we have said it seems to be the other face of the one that
makes infinite demands—or at least offers infinite criticisms.
If this is the destroyer-deconstructor who becomes a redeemer,
then I am even more puzzled, because it would seem that in
its transformation from one to the other, the infinite had to
negate its own infinity. If so, then the "infinite love" I just described would be changed to one that becomes finite, anthro-
pomorphic; but I am not sure where.

S: Perhaps in the finitude of the text, the Torah. That would account for the pleasure you receive—we all receive—from textual study.

B: Or also in the finitude of human faces—I mean the faces of
those with whom you study. We would find the interruption
and a reason to have faith in the task of interpreting the
other's face. Study itself is a gift, isn't it?

S: But Bob, what if we begin here, with love and not suffering?
Must we begin as you suggested with suffering, with negative
revelation? As postmodern Jewish philosophers, can't we also
begin with the text, with the Torah and *Gemara*, with God's
love letter to us? As you suggested awhile ago, Jewish postmoderns also have recourse to positive revelation—understood not as a universal revelation of truth, but as the Word
such as it was received by our particular, finite tradition and
community of discourse. If we take a hint from Rosenzweig
and begin with love—or as I see it, with the positive Jewish
revelation of the Torah—then we begin not only with resources of hope and faith that replenish our souls but also
with strategies of community, jurisprudence, and pedagogy to
face suffering—strategies that the deconstructive postmodern
philosophers lack.

Hermeneutics

B: Steve, in your definition, you wrote that "in recalling revelation as the written and oral Torah, I do not want to invoke the
fundamentalist notion that the Torah was given to Moshe at
Sinai; rather, I want to draw attention to the society-, law-, and
text-bound nature of revelation." But now you sound like you

are referring to a positive revelation as a set of laws? Are you saying we need to switch to a neo-Orthodox position?

S: No, I am not talking about the commandments. And I don't mean the dogma that the positive revelation was given at Sinai. I am interested, instead, in what the tradition gives us: the oral and the written Torah. We have texts; we have a teaching; we have continuous traditions of interpretation. We have something positive that teaches us—and the generic post-moderns don't have those kinds of resources. When I talk about the positive revelation, I am not claiming anything more authoritative than that these texts can serve as a basis for our philosophical reading and thinking. The Torah is a resource to replenish ourselves, but it also is a resource for learning how to address suffering.

B: I see the point about suffering—I would say that these texts interrupt us, challenge us, attune us to others' suffering.

P: But I would like to add that the Torah is a text that suffers, that suffers our reading and our not reading. The vulnerability of the text, its own need for our efforts, is part of its trusting relationship. But what do you mean about love—as opposed to suffering?

S: These texts are a source and inspiration of eros. They don't only make us hurt; they also bring us joy and make us love one another. You know how much passion is brought forth from these texts when we read the texts together. They excite our intellects and our passions. The text not only wounds us, it also is a Thou.

B: I would never want to deny the passions we share reading together. We all share that profound experience. But I don't think the text is a Thou. Maybe we need to talk about it in a different way. A Talmudic text is like a script for the performance of reading with another person. We take the parts of the various rabbis, trying to vindicate even those we don't agree with. We are made to take their parts. And the other person who sits across from me teaches me how to think about both my part and his or her own part. It is my partner who has to question my reading of the text. The partner is a You, but the text itself is not a Thou.

S: I am not trying to minimize the role of reading with another person, the community of reading. The Thou who reads with me teaches and challenges in a performative way. But let's not forget the specific role of these Jewish texts. Our sense of community does not form around reading just anything, but around the group of texts called "Torah" in Jewish tradition. These texts have a certain form, content, and authority and an ability to teach that makes them different from other texts. When we read philosophical texts, it is different from when we read Talmud. First, because we don't read philosophical books together; but also because those texts—even the texts of Plato—just do not generate the same kind of reading, the same kind of PJP community for us.

B: And that is because the rabbinic texts are dialogic. They ask us to take parts, and then they destabilize those parts by jumping from one context to another, changing the interlocutors. Even if every opinion is discarded, each one solicits the effort to justify it. You cannot read these texts alone; and when you read them with another person, they encourage you to improvise, to append your own thoughts, and to keep changing perspectives.

P: Postmodern Jewish philosophy looks to those texts to see the logic of that kind of reading: a logic of argumentation that examines a variety of contexts, that explores the range of vagueness, that does not totalize or dichotomize but displays the general in a dialogue among particular options. PJP reads rabbinic texts in order to pull out lessons for a postmodern logic.

S: I think we read Talmud because it addresses questions that philosophy abandoned: questions about God, about creation and revelation, about the value of a human life. The ultimate issues of our existence are addressed in the Talmud—and they are not solved. We turn from philosophical texts to Talmud in order to see the conflicting ways of thinking through important issues. That is why we love those texts. We address these texts as if they were a Thou—not literally a Thou, a living being, but like a Thou.

P: If you are speaking to anyone about anyone's reading, all right, then. Across community borders, we cannot demonstrate what God says, only that God has spoken. But within our community of reading Torah, we may indeed address the text as a Thou, for it is the vehicle of God's speaking directly to us.

B: What I would prefer is to think about how we address our partner as a Thou. We also relate to God through the text—but we come to God and find God through the text, through the linguistic product of our people's tradition. We relate to God through the text; to the other person before the text. God is not a Thou for us, and neither is the text. But only because of the text can we come near to God.

S: But that's the Shekhinah. I am not afraid to talk about the eros for God when we read the text of Torah—that God is present when two read Torah together.

B: No. It's only a trace of God. God leaves traces in the texts, and reading together illumines that the trace is a trace—because we also could miss it altogether. God does not show up—but the other person does.

P: But you both have just shifted from a conversation about the text to one about theology. Can you say something more about why your hermeneutic conversation just became theological?

S: Sure. We were beginning to find the theological dimension of *talmud torah*, of reading the Torah text together. It is not simply an intellectual or passionate experience—it is a liturgical performance. We can pray by reading together; it is a ritual relation with God.

P: May I ask: Is this, then, an activity that is limited to a particular community?

S: I think so. I mean, it is not liturgical when a group of philosophers meet to discuss Plato. The liturgical dimension requires Jewish texts, Torah. And that means it also requires Jewish readers.

B: I agree that Jewish texts strike a unique kind of relation; but Jewish texts also can speak to non-Jews, if they want to listen. Non-Jews can experience what you are calling the liturgical dimension of reading together.

P: They may, as anthropologists. But if we are talking about reading these texts, then we may have something to learn from the teaching in the Talmudic Tractate of Sanhedrin, that this level of reading may be achieved by a group of, say, nine Jews and one non-Jew, but not five and five.

S: That's from the same text that teaches about Akiva's martyrdom and loving God.

B: But that reminds me of the other Akiva story, where his death is a reward and is linked to his exegetical daring. Do you want to look at that text? The question is how he innovated and found more and more meaning in the materiality of the text itself. It's in *Menachot*. Peter, can you get the book?

P: Here it is. *Menachot* 29b.

> Rab Yehudah said in the name of Rab: When Moses ascended on high he found the Holy One, blessed be He, sitting, tying crownlets on letters. Moses said, "Master of the Universe, who stays your hand?"

B: Because it is "Rab Yehudah in the name of Rab," we know this story is told in Babylonia, several generations after Akiva's death. It shows that the later sages valued Akiva's role.

S: And Moses is impatient. He wants the Torah now. He is like a modern philosopher: He wants only the argument, the theme. He is not interested in the decoration, in the aspect of Torah that he cannot just say.

P: But God is busy with the ornamentation. The story indicates that we need the details, even the aspect of the graphemes that exceeds semantic meaning.

B: God is making a text, something not only to teach what has been said, but also a way of preserving the power of the text to say more.

> He answered, "There will be a man in the future, at the end of many generations, Akiva b. Joseph is his name. And he will interpret stroke by stroke, pile upon pile of laws."

S: God says that he needs interpreters. The ornamentation is an opening for the ongoing work of interpretation. Moses is not enough: The revelation of Torah requires a chance for later generations to renew the meaning.

B: Look at Akiva with his piles of laws. The Torah is not just a fixed set of commandments, it is a fruitful tree, a source of many rivers. This ongoing rush of commandments, leading beyond Moses's own work, but originating always in Moses's text—this is the way that a living legal tradition works.

S: That decoration of the text also makes the body of the Torah beautiful. Its beauty will draw us to it. This story is about aesthetics, too.

B: Not aesthetics. The beauty is the ornament, which provokes ongoing interpretation. But even if the biblical text opens and draws us after it like a beautiful object, the rabbinic texts are surprisingly not beautiful. They lack aesthetic unity and clarity of form.

S: Okay, it is not the beauty of a symmetrical mountain, it is a craggy coast. There are rocks everywhere, and it is so hard to navigate in them. And the lack of harmonious beauty has a hermeneutically productive value. It creates space for interpretation: "Moses said, 'Master of the Universe, show him to me.'"

S: Why does Moses want to see Akiva?

B: I don't know. Maybe Moses does not believe that anyone could interpret that way, that the text will open up that much?

S: Maybe Moses wants to learn the heap of laws—Moses did love the commandments and the promulgation of them.

B: Do you think Moses believes God?

S: Sure. But he has this "show me" attitude. He is curious.

B: He always wants to know. He wants to see someone actually interpreting those little scribbles.

S: But it's also like asking God to show God's glory. Moses wants to see.

B: That's the point: To see the text being interpreted is like seeing God's glory.

Such Torah, Such Reward!

Our dialogue ended here, but for the sake of completeness we present the rest of the story from Menachot:

He said, "Turn around behind you."

He [Moses] went and sat behind eight rows. He didn't understand what they were saying and was weak. But when they came to a matter, they said to their teacher, "Rabbi, where is this from?" He [Akiva] said to them, "It is a law of Moses from Sinai," [and] he [Moses] was comforted.

He returned before the Holy One, Blessed be He, and said, "Master of the Universe, You have a man like that and you give the Torah through me?"

He said, "Silence. Thus it came to my mind."

He said, "Master of the Universe, I have seen his teaching, show me his reward."

He said, "Turn around behind you."
He turned and saw them weighing his flesh in the slaughterhouse.
He said, "Master of the Universe, such Torah, such reward?"
He said, "Silence. Thus it came to my mind." (Menachot 29b)

NOTES

1. "So that the very phenomenon of suffering in its uselessness is, in principle, the pain of the Other. For an ethical sensibility—confirming itself, in the inhumanity of our time, against this inhumanity—the justification of the neighbour's pain is certainly the source of all immorality. Accusing oneself in suffering is undoubtedly the very turning back of the ego to itself. It is perhaps thus; and the for-the-other—the most upright relation to the Other—is the most profound adventure of subjectivity, its ultimate intimacy. But this intimacy can only be discrete. It could not be given as an example, or be narrated as an edifying discourse. It could not be made a predication without being perverted" (from E. Levinas, "Useless Suffering," in *The Provocation of Levinas,* eds. Robert Bernasconi and David Wood, trans. Richard Cohen [London: Routledge, 1988], p. 163).

2. Michael Fishbane, *The Garments of Torah: Essays in Biblical Hermeneutics* (Bloomington: Indiana University Press, 1989), pp. 27–28.

3. "The imperative of the commandment *[Gebot]* makes no provision for the future; it can only conceive the immediacy of obedience. If it were to think of a future or an Ever, it would be, not commandment nor order, but law *[Gesetz]*. Law reckons with times, with a future, with duration. The commandment knows only the moment; it awaits the result in the very instant of its promulgation" (Franz Rosenzweig, *The Star of Redemption,* trans. William W. Hallo [Boston: Beacon Press, 1971], p. 177; German ed. *Der Stern der Erlösung,* in *Franz Rosenzweig: Der Mensch und sein Werk, Gesammelte Schriften* [The Hague: Martinus Nijhoff, 1954], p. 197).

4. Levinas writes (the translation here is Gibbs's): "The other person is the very place of the metaphysical truth and is indispensable to my relation with God. He does not play the role of mediator. The other person is not the incarnation of God, but precisely by his face, where he is disincarnated, he is the manifestation of the height where God is revealed" (Emmanuel Levinas, *Totalité et Infini,* 4th ed. [The Hague: Martinus Nijhoff, 1971; 1st ed. 1961], p. 51; an alternative English translation may be found in Emmanuel Levinas, *Totality and Infinity,* trans. Alphonso Lingis [Pittsburgh, Pa.: Duquesne University Press, 1969], pp. 78–79).

5. Levinas writes (the translation here is Gibbs's): "The absolute experience is not disclosure but revelation: a coincidence of the expressed and the one who expresses, a showing, that is thereby the privileged one of the Other Person, showing a face beyond its form. Form incessantly betrays its

manifestation—congealing in plastic form since it is adequate to the Same, alienates the exteriority of the Other. The face is a living presence. It is expression. The life of expression consists in undoing its form, where the entity is exposed like a theme, dissimulating itself by the same. The face speaks. The showing of the face is already discourse" (*Ibid.*, pp. 37–38 [Fr. ed.], pp. 65–66 [Eng. ed.]).

Part Two

Commentary

4

Toward a Dialogic Postmodern Jewish Philosophy

Yudit Kornberg Greenberg

My response to this dialogue is a meditation on what members of this group have written as well as a continuation and an expansion of the questions I raised as a participant in the original dialogue. My comments consist of reflections on my role in the dialogue, followed by a discussion of the main characteristics of postmodern Jewish philosophy, which include: (1) the creation of a new philosophical community whose methodology is shaped by dialogic and textual reasoning; (2) the preeminence of Franz Rosenzweig's speech-thinking as a model and an influence for postmodern Jewish philosophy; (3) the concern for suffering and the protection of the other; (4) the integration of myth into theology, and the absorption of theological concepts into philosophy; (5) gender, eros, and love as categories of analysis in postmodern Jewish philosophy; (6) the critique of hierarchical thinking; and (7) the responsibility of interpreting/creating texts.

Our postmodern Jewish philosophy group was formed in 1992, when the four of us assembled with the purpose of striving together to reflect and discuss the parameters and meaning of our philosophical work and personal experiences. We were and still are creating for ourselves a space and a set of linguistic signs from and in which we could speak, affirming our identities as Jews, philosophers, men and women. In the course of our conversations, we discovered our shared beliefs as well as our differences. Our pains and joys also emerged and were reflected upon in the dialogue. As noted in the Introduction to this book, after our first conversation I was no longer able to attend our meetings, and I agreed to postpone my contributions to the discussion. Consequently, my role changed from that of participant to that of respondent.

What meaning can I derive from the changed role that I now occupy? My earlier contributions to the dialogue render me a partner in this dialogue. As a respondent, however, I am now "outside" the conversation, although still playing a role in the overall project. As an occupier of space both inside and outside the dialogue, I am privileged to reflect upon earlier statements and to "insert" my voice wherever I see fit. What effect did my absence have? The content of the discourse after my departure from the group signals that an important difference was lost (although other differences remained). As an Israeli woman, I represented a gender and a nationality *différance* in the group. Had I remained in the dialogue, I would have raised questions about issues that were ignored by my colleagues. For example, I would have brought up subjects such as embodiment, the representation of women, and hierarchical thinking in Jewish thought and philosophy. These subjects, which I have inserted later and in a monologic fashion (in this chapter), clearly would have altered our discourse.

The process of self-reflexivity challenges presuppositions of an abstract inquiry, of an objective subject in search of universality. It becomes clear that the presence or absence of certain interlocutors in the dialogue affects and alters the discourse. Thus, reflections on the personal can shed light on what in postmodern and feminist theory is referred to as the "location" (or "identity") of the speaker/thinker in his or her cultural context, socioeconomic position, and gender. These aspects of individual or personal "uniqueness" also might commonly be shared by a number of persons (even though those persons differ from one another in other important respects), and thus can "locate" a group as well as an individual. A central "location" for our group is its members' common objective of creating a new community through dialogue: We came together to articulate our various experiences and desires as scholars/philosophers and as Jews, hoping that in the process we would solidify as a community— as an alternative community of specifically Jewish philosophers and thinkers.

Although we all agree with the vision of reading Jewish texts together and of emulating Talmudic conversations, our dialogue points to hermeneutical, and more importantly, ideological *différance,* which leads us to ask: What is the logic of this kind of reading?

What are the theological, social, and political dimensions of reading texts together? There is a debate among my colleagues on two fundamental issues. The first issue is whether the text is our Thou or is the medium that opens us to the Thou with whom we share the text. Text-centeredness is called into question if it leaves out the human partnership, the human "I-Thou." Although these two claims are not mutually exclusive, they do point us in different directions. The second issue is the placement of suffering in our inquiry. This issue engages us in the link between our concern for contemporary topics of suffering and our passion for the classical sources of Judaism.

I agree with the vision and objective of creating a human partnership around a text. I would emphasize that the central issue for us is that of agency. In other words, what texts we study is secondary to the question of *how* we study them. We have assumed the responsibility to avoid the totalizing practices of our forebears in this century (see my comments below on the Holocaust) and the subversive practices of our rabbinic forebears who sought to eliminate women's voices or objectify them.

I would further underscore that in our post-Holocaust era, there is a great existential urgency to move the idea of dialogue as originally conceived by dialogic philosophers in new and important directions.[1] Our new direction is to put this philosophy into *action*. This move is profound, for it is a social/political act: Beyond the production of additional scholarship on dialogue, we have here the creation of an alternative intellectual discourse and community.[2] Our premise and inspiration is the creation of a community based on the shared reading of texts. This existential return to Jewish texts is inspired by Franz Rosenzweig, whose return to a full Jewish life was grounded in the study of classical texts. His enthusiastic embrace of Jewish scholarship is evident also in his rejection of a university career for the sake of directing the Lehrhaus, a school in Frankfurt devoted to adult Jewish education.

Rosenzweig is the preeminent precursor to postmodern Jewish philosophy both in his method of dialogic thinking and in his turn or return to Jewish texts. Rosenzweig's unapologetic celebration of Jewish myths, symbols, and rituals is indicative of his break from his assimilated German Jewish culture, as well as his break with and profound critique of traditional philosophy. This is evident in the philosophical shifts found in *The Star of Redemption*. Instead of bringing Judaism to the pale of philosophy, even to empirical or dialogic philosophy, Rosenzweig reversed the modernist trend and brought philosophy and theology to the world of Jewish text and experience. Against the backdrop of modernist demythologization, he remythologized the truth of creation, revelation, and redemption in light of biblical and midrashic landscapes. Finally, his devotion to Jewish texts can be seen in the transformation of his later scholarship from abstract philosophical discourse to translations and commentaries to the Torah and to Yehudah Halevi's poetry.

Following Rosenzweig's basic theory of speech-thinking, a characteristic of postmodern Jewish philosophy is dialogue as the medium for doing philosophy. The vision here is of dialogic relationships created in a community of philosophers who gather together to study traditional Jewish texts. In contrast with Hegelian dialectic reading, which severs the sense of continuity between historical periods, we wish to read previous texts with humility and careful listening. We criticize as oppressive the modernist tendency to generalize a particular tradition. Rather, we aim to create a dialogic relationship that emphasizes polysemic readings, and continuity between historical periods and texts.

Our Jewishness is not only our point of departure; Jewish teachings are also our companion. We embrace, albeit in a critical and suspicious fashion, the centrality of Torah in Jewish life. An important impetus in our return to Jewish sources is our disillusionment with modernist philosophical tendencies. Against a modernist tendency to absolutize the self, we seek to place the absolute outside the self.

How do we synthesize our retrieval of classical Jewish texts with our attentiveness to issues of suffering and the quest for the good? Initially, it would seem that both classical texts and the Holocaust call us back to premodern particularism. Our commitment to wrestle with the particularities of Jewish existence, especially Jewish suffering, should not, however, be seen as antithetical to the modernist quest for goodness. It is through our return to our heritage that we recover our sense of goodness. However, this quest for goodness does not entail ignoring our particularities, as it has for modern philosophers.

The second issue that we debated and the question that still haunts us is: Do we begin studying texts with love and joy, or with suffering? Even though this is a question of beginnings, it is linked to content and context, and more specifically, to the question of the Holocaust. We all agree that the Holocaust is a marker for us, but is it our starting point or our focus? We disagree here on our relations to history—Ochs insists that the postmodern is not a historical marker; rather, it is a way of thinking. Gibbs, on the other hand, states that the Holocaust is a starting point for postmodern Jewish philosophy. Kepnes, too, agrees that after the Holocaust, Jewish thought cannot be divorced from history.

Inspired by the philosophy of Levinas, the trope of the face offers us three symbolic points of reference: the face of the child, who demands finitely; the face of the suffering stranger with infinite demands; finally, the face that offers infinite love. We are inclined toward wrestling with the centrality and the narrative of suffering. A distinction between Jewish and other postmodern thinking should be made here. In contrast with Derridean deconstruction, which is essentially a model of interrupted speech, Jewish postmodernism should be primarily a constructionist effort.[3] Following the rabbinic model of rebuilding, we wish to give birth to the process of transformation from negative interruption to positive speech. This is nothing other than the logic and process of redemption.

I agree with my partners regarding the primary role that should be given to evil and suffering in postmodern Jewish philosophy. Indeed, how could we ignore these subjects after the Holocaust? However, my colleagues' response to evil and suffering is essentially discursive. Had I been there at this point of our dialogue, I would have pressed for exploring other modes of thinking after the Holocaust. For me, turning to mythic thinking is a profound way of addressing evil and suffering. We have in Jewish history numerous types of response to evil and suffering. Lurianic thought, for example, with its mythic formulation of suffering, exile, and redemption, was born approximately seventy years after the expulsion from Spain. I suggest that the power of myth might help us cope with our spiritual vacuity and have transforming consequences at this post-Holocaust historical/intellectual juncture.

Lurianic visions and terminology, for example, are helpful in giving meaning to the reality of catastrophe, destruction, loss, and alienation in our postmodern condition. Not only cosmological theories but also the mystic's testimony to the inner life and his/her metaphoric construction of truth are significant signposts for the spiritual dimensions of reality. What we need now is not a theology of despair but a theology of hope.

Arthur Green poses an important question relevant to this problem: How do we move to a position of spiritual affirmation in the face of the absurd world that post-Holocaust theologian Richard Rubenstein has portrayed for us?[4] Referring to Rabbi Nachman of Bratslav, who reappropriated the Lurianic idea of *tsimtsum*, Green explicates the powerful mythic resource of the kabbalah and its contemporary, post-Holocaust theological implications. *Tsimtsum*, or God's self-withdrawal from the world, translates into the absence of God from certain levels of reality. In order to create the world, God had to withdraw from it. This concept introduces the notion of three levels of consciousness, the first being the level of simple piety, filled with God's presence. As we go deeper, we reach the second level of *tsimtsum*, where God in fact does not exist. In this second level of consciousness, we confront the void through probing and doubt—in other words, through rational thinking. If we continue beyond this level of darkness, devoid of God's presence, we will reach the third level of consciousness, the level of God's reappearance manifested through faith and love. Nachman's reworking of Lurianic theory is an illustration of how mythic thinking can help us wrestle with a particularly devastating event such as the Holocaust.

Another example of a "useful" mystical theory for us is the Lurianic conception of redemption. In opposition to mainstream views of redemption as messianic—a historical march forward—the kabbalists and the Lurianic school in particular understand the messianic path as restoring the world to its original harmony and unity. What is particularly compelling about this vision is the process by which the redemption of the world would occur. This process, known as *tikkun olam*, or the restitution of the world, is based on both an individualistic and cosmic view of redemption and the centrality of humanity's role in repairing and redeeming the world. *Tsimtsum, tikkun olam*, and other Lurianic myths are paradigmatic for our philosophy, for we are open to imaginative forms of thinking, especially as we struggle with the classical problem of theodicy.

In addition to this effort to remythologize our theology, I would locate another trend in postmodern Jewish philosophy. Emerging from Rosenzweig, we could articulate it as the absorption of theological language into philosophy or the blurring of the rigid distinctions between philosophy and theology. Rosenzweig reflected on the relations between philosophy and theology in his essay "The New Thinking." He suggested that philosophers who were commonly identified with the dialogic method were concerned, among other things, with theological issues. He stated what he thought should be the nexus of the two methods/disciplines: "Theological problems must be translated into human terms, and human problems brought into the pale of theology."[5]

To apply Rosenzweig's own attempt to integrate theology and philosophy, we find in the center of his philosophical work concepts such as creation, revelation, and redemption. Although these have traditionally been seen as the domain of theology, Rosenzweig rethought them as truth-claims integral to his new thinking. As such, these enabled him to articulate his views of the relational self and the production of meaning. Hermeneutic and phenomenological methodologies are employed and can be further deployed in an explication of his discourse. The religious category of revelation, for example, provides Rosenzweig a conceptual framework from which to elaborate not only the relationship between revelation and tradition but also a theory of language, focusing on the problematics of the hierarchical order of speech and writing.

The linking of philosophy and theology can also be understood as a broader attempt to overcome disciplinary boundaries, as Rosenzweig himself had done in the third part of the *Star*, where sociology of religion, for example, is brought to bear upon theology. His theological model brings to light how theological categories are not constructed in a vacuum but arise from and give voice and meaning to social practices. Rosenzweig's study of Christian liturgy and culture in parallel to Jewish practices and in accordance with his paradigm of creation, revelation, and redemption is a fine example of the relaxation of rigid definitions of theological discourse.

An essential feature of postmodern Jewish philosophy should be the challenge against hierarchical modes of thinking that pit sexuality against spirituality, mind against body, male against female, rational discourse against myth and poetry, and ethics against metaphysics. If I were present during our discussions, I would have addressed hierarchical thinking by articulating questions related to embodiment and temporality, especially questions of gender and sexuality.

The category of gender is a central objective for us in studying, analyzing, or appropriating classical Jewish texts, given the history of male authorship and patriarchal values that shaped these texts. One of the current debates revolves around the recovery and appropriation of feminine imagery from ancient texts. This is particularly a problem in those mystical or midrashic texts that are rich in gender symbolism. Positively, a philosophy/theology that draws on such symbolic structures should combat false dichotomies and produce more inclusive paradigms of knowledge than those afforded by traditional models of thought.

However, this move to recover feminine symbolism must be made carefully. First, we must examine this rich interpretive/intellectual history against the backdrop of the social conditions of women in Jewish history. Furthermore, we must critically analyze the meaning of the feminine within the various symbolic structures that our scribes, rabbis, kabbalists, and philosophers have erected.[6] In Jewish mysticism, we often find that the feminine is subsumed into the masculine and is not an independent entity that can provide a genuine source of feminine/feminist empowerment.

I would also urge us to pay close attention to eros and representations of the body in the classical sources. The uncovering and recovering of eros is the explication of our deepest desires, fears, and longings, as well as those of the authors of classical Jewish texts, erotic and spiritual alike, as these are evidenced and manifested in our readings/writings and in theirs. Hermeneutic questions such as the relationship between eros and allegory (not only in the *Song of Songs* but also in other erotic religious texts) press us to confront the tension between sexuality and spirituality.

A study of the depiction of love in Jewish thought—a study that views love both independently of and in relation to eros—further undermines traditional dualistic and hierarchical thought patterns like the mind/body dualism.[7] In the writings of Moses Maimonides, for example, love and gender often play the role of the extrarational: The masculine is valorized as rational, over and against the emotions and the "feminine" discourses of poetry and myth. Yehudah Halevi in the medieval period, Judah Abrabanel in the early modern period, and Rosenzweig in the modern period offer an alternative to the dominant, rationalist mode of discourse—an alternative that affirms sensuality and the poetic.

In these various ways, postmodern Jewish philosophy can be said to be a form of *tikkun,* a healing of past wounds and hierarchical thinking. I envision a reconfiguration of the relationship between mind and body, sexuality and spirituality, rational discourse and its others (poetry, myth) and between ethics and metaphysics. I hope that we shall continue our work with greater awareness of the truth that myth-/textmaking is a social and political practice. Indeed, our challenge as an emerging postmodern Jewish philosophical community is not only to grasp the fallibility of our forefathers but in humility and care, to take responsibility for our own.

NOTES

1. The main principle of dialogic philosophy is the insistence on the relational self and the irreducibility of the other to the same. In his essay "The New Thinking," Rosenzweig refers to Ludwig Feuerbach as the first thinker to discover dialogic thinking. Other thinkers commonly identified in this philosophical tradition include Martin Buber and Ferdinand Ebner.

2. It is noteworthy that a central goal for us has been to strengthen our sense of community through regular meetings and conversations. These meetings are structured on the model of rabbinic *chevruta* (study partners). This type of discourse is emblematic of the reasoning and the dialogic process that we wish to reclaim.

3. Deconstructionism, the most prominent practitioner of which is Jacques Derrida, is founded on the belief that the objective approach to reality is not possible, and seeks to undermine any attempt to create a coherent philosophical system and social structures. The constructionist perspective, on the other hand, although it is similarly critical of modernism's assumptions of objectivity, nevertheless seeks to create a new speech that would provide meaning and sustain hope in the possibility of goodness.

4. Arthur Green, "The Role of Jewish Mysticism in a Contemporary Theology of Judaism." *Shefa Quarterly*, vol. 1, pp. 25–40.

5. Franz Rosenzweig, "The New Thinking," in N. Glatzer, *Franz Rosenzweig* (New York: Schocken, 1976), p. 201. As an example, Rosenzweig considers the problem of the name of God, which is only part of the problem of the logic of names in general. Another, more idiosyncratic example relates to the validity of investigating aesthetics from the perspective of whether or not artists may attain salvation.

6. The work of Elliot Wolfson, Daniel Boyarin, and Howard Eilberg-Schwarz, for example, pioneers contemporary text scholarship illuminating sexist practices of feminine imageries. For analysis of gender in Jewish philosophy, see the essay by Susan Shapiro, "A Matter of Discipline: Reading for Gender in Jewish Philosophy," in *Judaism Since Gender*, edited by Miriam Peskowitz and Laura Levitt (New York and London: Routledge, 1997).

7. I am currently working on a book-length manuscript that treats the subject of eros in relationship to love in Jewish thought.

5

Toward a Postmodern Judaism: A Response

Susan E. Shapiro

The invitation to participate in this conversation is one that I happily accept. In doing so, I'd like to note first that my use of postmodernism has primarily been in my intellectual work, specifically in the reading of contemporary critical theory, and not—as here—as a form of cultural, political, or communal practice or identification. And so my accepting this invitation to respond to the dialogue entails my entering its not strictly intellectual terrain. The efficacy of such a dialogue depends in large measure on the quality and commitment of the partners in conversation, and on that score this enterprise has much to recommend it. Further, while its title announces that the dialogue concerns "postmodern Jewish philosophy," in many respects its subject seems significantly broader: "Jewish postmodernism." Formulated thus, the two terms are juxtaposed, their order of priority remaining ambiguous or suspended. A series of questions can then be raised that might help to further locate the subject of the dialogue: Is the subject under discussion postmodernism, with Jewishness added, or is postmodernism treated here as the supplement of Jewishness or Judaism? Of course, one could quickly respond that this question is undecidable. And certainly, each term might alter the sense of the other through their juxtaposition. Such interpenetration might generally predominate in this dialogue; but at other times it seems that one term or the other is granted priority. And which term—"Jewishness" (and "Judaism") or "postmodernism"—is taken as more primary and constitutive, and in what context, bears important consequences. In the following remarks, as I engage a number of issues and themes that arise within and from the discussion among Bob, Peter, Steven, and Yudit, I also note how the two basic terms of this conversation—"Judaism," or "Jewishness," and "postmodernism"—have been differently defined and weighted and with what consequences.

Other respondents to the dialogue have situated it within the context of contemporary postmodern theories and thought. Still others have reviewed the many salient moments and topics of the dialogue. I have, therefore, decided to take a different tack. I will enter the dialogue by beginning with specific lacunae and problems I have found within the text. In some cases, I will bring in references to contemporary postmodern and critical theories in order to articulate these issues further. In other cases, I will respond more directly to these gaps and problems.

The main topics I will address in this essay are: (1) "I can imagine what a feminist would say"; (2) circumcision and the immemorial; (3) thinking about the Holocaust; and (4) toward postmodern communities. There were many other subjects that could have been singled out, but these are the four that struck me most and that seemed to strongly call for a response. By addressing these issues, not necessarily in the order of their appearance in the initial conversation, I will begin to articulate what I think are the stakes of Jewish postmodernism and why. In this way, finally, I hope both to critique and to further the dialogue.

"I Can Imagine What a Feminist Would Say"

This statement appears in the section on "Suffering, and the Other's Freedom." It is a musing, however, that could well apply to nearly all of the dialogue. Although the remark "I can imagine what a feminist would say" importantly registered the lack of feminist intervention at this point in the conversation, it provoked for me the sense of the general absence of women's voices in the dialogue. While not all women, certainly, are feminists and not all feminists are women, this phrase does throw a spotlight on a significant lacuna in the dialogue. In the following, I would like to begin by clearing a space for feminist response. In order to do so, however, I will first draw attention to where women's voices are absent from the main body of the dialogue. In this way, I hope to extend a meditation on a very important yet unrealized dimension of the text and possibility of the dialogue.

The character of the absence/presence of women in this postmodern dialogue brings to mind yet another dialogue, that of Plato's *Symposium*. It evokes for me both the image of the flute girl—that fleeting figure who serves wine to the men in the symposium and who then disappears from the scene of the dialogue—and that of Diotima, interpolated by Socrates, who as David Halperin suggests, appropriates her speech in and for a discourse between men. In this interpolation, Socrates "cross-dresses" as a woman and thereby obscures the woman herself (Diotima).[1] Socrates "reimagines what a woman said" in his invocation of Diotima's authority through the ventrilocution of her views and speech in the dialogue.[2]

As in the *Symposium*, the absence of women's voices in the dialogue about postmodernism has consequences, some of which will be addressed in the next section of my response (on circumcision and the immemorial). And it raises the further critical problem of the relationship of my discourse as "commentary" or "response" to this text: What is the status of my remarks in relation to the text of the dialogue? What does it mean that I am speaking after? Doesn't all commentary, by definition, come after that to which it responds? Should I refrain from remarking upon the absence of women's voices in the text and instead treat issues that don't bear on this problem? What difference, if any, does gender make for the relation of text and commentary? Are my comments—like the flute girl—merely fleeting addenda to an already formed initial dialogue? Or can commentary and response open a space in the text of the dialogue for intervention and reorientation?

One way of creating feminist space through commentary would be something of a master/slave inversion: The commentaries would displace topographically the texts they were commenting on, with the original dialogue being located in the margins and corners surrounding the now central commentaries. This inversion, furthermore, would problematize the relation between the first dialogue and its supplemental commentaries in a way that would resonate with other postmodern discourses. But my response is coming after. A simple inversion would likely have reproduced the gender politics of the text, "upside down." Even so, such an inversion is important because of its implications for the politics of gender relations; at least it raises the question of this ordering and its consequences.

As I have noted, one of these consequences is the character of the discussion about circumcision, which I discuss below. Another issue is the notion of "community" that develops throughout the dialogue, which I discuss in the fourth section of this response. And yet, it is important to note that I have been invited to participate—albeit in a kind of afterword—in the larger, extended dialogue. Others might claim that commentary is akin to "having the last word." But that is precisely what a dialogue, especially a postmodern one, may not have or enact. Although I have their text (excised and amended, a revision already functioning as a kind of silent commentary constituting the "original" dialogue), I do not have Bob's, Peter's, Steve's, or Yudit's response to my words. Nor can the readers' responses to this volume be anticipated. While there is an absence of women's voices in the heart of this dialogue, an invitation significantly has been extended and accepted. The responses that occur beyond and outside of the text of the dialogue and those of its four respondents will, likewise, be an acceptance of a further invitation to join in and extend this dialogue about "postmodern Judaism."[3] I hope that my remarks will have in some measure facilitated further feminist participation and intervention in this extended dialogue.

Circumcision and the Immemorial

Yudit's presence made an important difference for the focus and character of the dialogue. When she was no longer able to be present, her absence was notable and the tone of the conversation changed. I imagine that it would have been a rather different dialogue had Yudit been able to participate in all of the discussions. Somewhere in the middle of the dialogue, after Yudit had left, Steven, Bob, and Peter began a riff on circumcision, castration, Jews, Greeks, covenant, and manhood. Circumcision is receiving increased attention of late, especially among male scholars of Jewish studies, some of whom warrant their interest as analogous to feminist concerns expressed by women. Some postmodern thinkers—prominent among them Jacques Derrida—have also become interested in the sign of circumcision as a way of ambivalently engaging their Jewishness.[4] One of the persistent themes in these discussions is the relationship of, or the insistent difference between, circumcision and castration. For example, the feminization of the Jewish male in modern discourse is both registered and resisted in Freud's writings, is appraised in some contemporary Freud scholarship on circumcision and the male Jew's body,[5] and is reappraised by others.[6] This reappraisal embraces a return to a positive evaluation of the limiting of virility or machismo that circumcision (as opposed to castration) represents. The gentle Talmud scholar becomes the model of Jewish manhood for Daniel Boyarin, just as the infinite responsibility of one individual for another becomes, for Emmanuel Levinas, the ethic made possible by the "circumcision" (the limiting of the virility) of the subject.[7] Derrida's treatment of circumcision as the inescapable sign of the particularism of Jewish manhood reproduces the debates of the Enlightenment in which Jews, in particular, were understood to be particularistic—especially as evidenced by the intransigence of *that* sign. Derrida's ruminations on his Jewishness are connected by him to circumcision and to both his mother and death. This is not an accidental connection. It is of a piece with the involuntary. One does not choose one's mother, nor do we usually understand death as something freely chosen—to the extent that we could choose something we do not know.[8] And like the parents we happen to have, however fortunate we may be in this accident of our birth, and like death, circumcision also is not understood as freely chosen.[9] Nor is Derrida's Jewishness freely chosen. It is confronted after the fact. Indeed, Derrida writes as if his Jewishness were determined by the very fact of his having been circumcised.

Most of the discussion among Bob, Peter, and Steve on circumcision focused on the question of its representational force—material/literal or spiritual/allegorical. However, I think that beyond the more obvious currency of this topic (especially for Jewish men) is a profound question: the question of the involuntary, or—following Levinas and Jean-François Lyotard, what I would prefer to call "the Immemorial."[10] And this Immemorial is that of the Brit, or covenant.[11] Circumcision for Jewish men is an inscription in the flesh—and not only the heart as spirit—because what is being enacted is a covenant that is Immemorial. That is, the Brit is known as already binding upon a Jew before his choosing whether or not to follow its dictates. But this covenant, this agreement between God and Abraham or between God and the Jewish people, can never itself be "remembered" except as the Immemorial idea that conditions present choice.[12] This is *not* a modern choice eventuating in the formation of individual autonomy. It is, rather, for Levinas, a postmodern "difficult freedom" that infinitely binds the individual in obligation to the other. It is "postmodern" in the nonchronological sense indicated by Lyotard in his consideration of Montaigne as postmodern.[13] It is also postmodern in the sense that it offers a critique of modernity and modernism, specifically of the notions of freedom and responsibility derived from the reciprocal (if mythical) social contract between equals. The covenant here is and is not entered into freely. It is an "agreement" freely entered into, in which one recognizes that one is always already obligated. It is the sign of circumcision that reminds one (i.e., the male Jew) of this immemorial obligation.

Why is circumcision of the heart alone not sufficient for the Jew? This, of course, is an age-old "differend,"[14] as the discourses of Paul and the rabbis make clear. But circumcision of the flesh—including but going beyond that of the heart or spirit—is necessary, in a Levinasian approach, if one (again, the male Jew) is to "re-member" the Immemorial. "Re-membering" the covenant (the Immemorial, always, already obligation to the Other) is enacted through doing mitzvot. It is not only a "memory" that the Torah was given or the covenant enacted. It is a "memory" of an obligation taken on by our ancestors, in which we, as their descendants, are also obligated. And this obligation can only be "re-membered" through the enacting of the covenant itself, through the doing of mitzvot. This circularity is a sign of the always already, transcendental character of the covenant as Immemorial. This impossible memory can only be "re-called" as preceding us, as calling to us from the past—a past, however, that can never be made immediate. For this is a past in which there was a covenant with God, of which we have (at least) two evident traces: the text of the Torah and the mark of circumcision.[15] The text ceaselessly calls for interpretation; circumcision—that seemingly most tangible and telling of signs—is a sign of what cannot be re-presented. Without such a physical re-marking, would the infinitely prior Immemorial be "remembered" as such and as always already obligating us? There is something inescapable about this mark of the Immemorial, the infinitely obligating covenant, made and (except for the case of adult male conversion) inscribed on the eighth day of a Jewish boy's life. Before memory, this sign of the Immemorial is made tangible, ever evidently present.

I use the term "we" here because I speak as a Jew. But I also speak as a Jewish woman. As such, I am not subject to this mitzvah. And so, although I've certainly noticed the increased interest of some of my male Jewish colleagues in writing and talking about circumcision, I can only speculate as to their (different) investments. Some certainly experience, or at least, interpret, circumcision as a kind of heteronomous violence (hence its affiliation with castration). It is understood by some as a sacrifice or as an oedipal drama of an *Akedah* in which the father reenacts the violence done to him, revisiting it on his son.[16] For others, it evokes the othering and/or feminizing of the Jewish male by the gaze of the non-Jew. Being "discovered" to be circumcised almost invariably meant death in Nazi Europe. It was an inescapable sign of being singled out. Against one's will. For some, being made to bear the visible sign of being Jewish before one can choose to be or not to be constitutes a violent chosenness. Further, living in an anti-Semitic world in which Jewish difference is pathologized exacerbates this sense of helplessness.

And yet, for some contemporary thinkers, this very vulnerability— usually associated with the "feminine" and the state of women— seems to open certain possibilities.[17] To say that Israel is God's bride and that this trope is central for the covenant, amplifies some of these associations.[18] Some of these associations sexualize circumcision. And certainly, this metaphor sets up a gender system that has had hierarchies of governance of soul over body and male over female mapped onto it.[19] However, this fact does not make circumcision a figure of Jewishness applicable only to men, as Jay Geller has persuasively shown in the case of Rachel Varnhagen.[20] To say that a Jewish man is "reminded" by circumcision of the Immemorial (just as a skullcap reminds him of God) is not to say that a Jewish woman cannot "remember" the Immemorial or God because she is not subject to circumcision. It is also, however, not to say that it is insignificant that the Brit is a ritual of entry into the covenant for which there is no traditional analogue for baby girls.[21]

When men talk about circumcision with other men, they risk reproducing the dynamics of an exclusively male ritual in which women look on, or more typically, choose not to watch. While one may legitimate such discourse by terming it a "men's group" activity, there are other styles of discourse in which such speech could mark male difference and yet invite women into the conversation as partners and participants in the covenant.[22] One way to accomplish this is not to get overly, indeed fetishistically, focused on where this sign is marked, while addressing the importance of this location.[23] I do not mean to suggest that this is easy. But I think that there are some significances that can be recovered by a refusal to be overly literal without effacing the importance of the literal—the sign made in the flesh, as opposed to the allegorical sign of the spirit. And equally importantly, women can be included in this nonfetishistic conversation in which the subject has been refashioned, for it is the Immemorial that is at stake in this marking. Again, why is circumcision of the heart not considered sufficient for Jews? The physical sign is *also* needed, not to replace the spiritual circumcision of the heart, but because "forgetting" the Immemorial (or forgetting to "remember" the Immemorial) is so easy and such a temptation.[24] For how does one "remember" what one cannot by definition remember: that which is in the "always already" and yet makes a claim upon one, to which one is responsible?[25]

Thinking About the Holocaust

I believe that theological response to the Shoah is crucial to contemporary Jewish thought and identity. This is not to say that particular responses have not been subject to parochialism and even a certain kitschiness. But taking unfortunate instances of post-Holocaust thought as exemplary of all responses to the Shoah is, in my opinion, irresponsible—that is, lacking in responsibility to the suffering of the other person(s). The point, as I see it, is not for us to focus on the vicarious suffering of those of us who were not there but to respond to the actual suffering of those who were. This, I take it, is also Bob's main concern throughout the section of the dialogue on this subject: that is, with attending to the suffering of the *other* person. How one regards the Shoah and its place in contemporary philosophical or theological writing, however, cannot be dictated. The discomfort that some of the dialogue participants seemed to have with focusing in any way on the event and its aftermath is something that they probably cannot be argued out of. It is clear that the discussion of the Shoah in the dialogue evoked strong passions. Perhaps these passions were motivated by a fear that Judaism and Jewishness will be overtaken by that event—that our long history, heritage, and traditions will all be reduced and made insignificant in light of the magnitude of the Shoah. It is as if by remembering the Holocaust one might risk forgetting Judaism and Jewishness.

To the extent that this is a threat, I can sympathize with those who worry about "overemphasizing" the Shoah. But I would suggest that the issue is not one of selective attention, of only seeing the Shoah and of being blinded by its magnitude. I think that both Jews and non-Jews have had genuine philosophical and theological questions raised by the Holocaust. These questions are better addressed than suppressed. Furthermore, they can become openings for engaging critically with a tradition—Jewish, Christian, or Muslim—in a way that might fairly be characterized as postmodern as well as post-Holocaust. It is important, however, not to conflate postmodern and post-Holocaust writing and thought.[26]

In the context of this connecting and differentiating between post-Holocaust discourse and postmodernism, I would like to bring up again—but differently—the concept of the Immemorial. The Immemorial cannot be represented. Likewise, the claim that the Holocaust cannot be adequately described, expressed, or understood is by now a commonplace. It has often been associated with the writings of Elie Wiesel; but the nonrepresentability of the "disaster" is also a prevalent trope in French postmodern discourse.[27] But in these latter discourses, the nonrepresentability of the Shoah and that of the immemorial past are entwined, equated, even identified. The Shoah as the historical Immemorial is, in different ways, subsumed under and absorbed by the transcendental Immemorial. However, the inability to represent the immemorial past, which by definition we cannot remember but which conditions us and always already binds and obligates us, is not identical with the claim that all representations of the Shoah are intrinsically inadequate to the task. Much, of course, depends on what one means by "(in)adequate." But deferring this question for the moment, I would like to focus on critically pulling apart, and then relating again, these two Immemorials.[28]

The transcendental Immemorial for Levinas, as I have already suggested, infinitely obligates the one to the other, me to the other person. The infinite character of this obligation is evident in its always already preceding me. This infinite obligation is the "difficult freedom" about which Levinas teaches us. As I have already suggested, this obligation is founded not in the autonomous freedom of the self but in the heteronomous and infinite obligation of the self to the other person. It is in part this ethics of post-autonomy that makes Levinas's thought postmodern. This critique of autonomy as the starting point for ethics is, importantly, a post-Holocaust intervention as well, one that in part provoked Levinas's return to the resources of Judaism. For it was precisely the failure in the Shoah of the ethics of identification that led to the other's near extermination. In order to respond to this catastrophic failure of modernity, Levinas takes us, as it were, infinitely "back" to the transcendental Immemorial and "beyond," toward the infinitely other and our (infinite) obligation, evoked by the "face" of the other person.[29] This may be understood as a kind of *tikkun* for another (not transcendental, but historical) Immemorial, for the disregard and destruction of the "face" in the Shoah. The character of the historical Immemorial and of the Shoah is crucial to Levinas, even though it appears only in traces throughout his writings. His postmodern critique of autonomy is deeply informed by the Shoah as well as by other genocides of the twentieth century. One could argue that traces of *l'univers concentrationnaire* (the concentrational universe) can be found in the concept of *il y a*, the excessiveness of the "there is" in which the self is utterly submerged. This universe also could be understood to be present in the radical disregard of the "face" of the other person. Seeing and hearing the nakedness and the vulnerability of the face of the other person is a habitus, a training that reintroduces the ethical into a world turned catastrophic. Levinas does not skip over the Shoah, even if he does not—in my opinion— focus sufficiently on its immemorial character or on its difference from and relation to the transcendental Immemorial.[30]

Toward Postmodern Communities

A desire was expressed at the beginning of the dialogue and was described as having occasioned its undertaking—the desire for a postmodern community in which one might feel at home. The partners in the dialogue evidenced a deep sense of the lack of such a community. The feeling of "homelessness" expressed by the dialogue partners was interpreted by them as a form of alienation to be overcome, even if such alienation is, indeed, part of the postmodern condition. Judaism and its emphasis on close, face-to-face communities was regarded in the dialogue as a kind of antidote to this alienation. But what, then, of the state of postmodern Judaism or postmodern Jewishness? Is postmodernism the problematic condition that Judaism could, in principle, resolve? Or is Judaism itself rendered postmodern, as seemingly attested by the lack of a "community of one's own," felt so strongly by the dialogue partners?

What if postmodernism is understood as a valid form of dwelling rather than as a problem? What if the sense of estrangement felt in any community is understood as the experience of being only partially "at home" in any given communal arrangement?[31] And what of the desire to have all our spiritual and other needs fulfilled under one roof? What opportunities for community are instead opened up by dwelling between communities, between alternative ways of being Jewish, between ways of being?

I am aware that the desire for a single postmodern Jewish community in which one would feel fully at home, with all one's complexity and contradictions, is a great temptation and is very hard to give up. But I am concerned that this desire could block the realization that one can live through and across differences within and between multiple identities and communities. The version of "postmodern Judaism" that would emerge from this latter realization would refuse to reify either term. It would allow for a kind of heterology and difference that the quest for one exclusive home does not. In such a living between as well as within various communities, one would be enabled to dwell as both a feminist and a Jew, for example, without truncating either.

I do not mean to suggest that such a "living between" is easy. But I do think it is commensurate with a certain rigorous diasporic Jewish identity that does not seek to erase the "differends" within the self or between communities. Furthermore, it might be possible in this way to live a form of "postmodern Judaism" or "postmodern Jewishness" that is not subject to or regulated by a desire for homogeneity as the condition or sign of community. Finally, such a postmodern mode of dwelling in tradition and community might importantly offer an alternative to the increasingly militant drawing of boundaries between the various branches of Judaism that emerged in—and in response to—modernity.[32]

NOTES

1. See David M. Halperin, "Why Is Diotima a Woman? Platonic *Eros* and the Figuration of Gender," in David M. Halperin, John J. Winkler, and Froma I. Zeitlin, eds., *Before Sexuality: The Construction of Erotic Experience in the Ancient World* (Princeton: Princeton University Press, 1990), pp. 257–308.

2. Following Halperin's emphasis on the absence of Diotima from the *Symposium*, even her invention by Socrates for the purposes of his discourse, we might here rather say, Socrates "imagines what a woman would say." See, in this regard, especially Halperin, "Why Is Diotima a Woman,"

pp. 292–298. For another important reading of Diotima that emphasizes her absence/presence in the dialogue, see Luce Irigaray, "Sorcerer Love: A Reading of Plato's *Symposium*, Diotima's Speech," in Nancy Tuana, ed., *Feminist Interpretations of Plato* (University Park: Pennsylvania State University Press, 1994), pp. 180–195 (originally published as "L'amour sorcier: Lecture de Platon *Le Banquet*, Discours de Diotime," in Luce Irigaray, *Ethique de la différence sexuelle* [Paris: Editions de Minuit, 1984]). For a critique of Irigaray as misreading Plato's, Socrates's, and Diotima's views on love, see Andrea Nye, "Irigaray and Diotima at Plato's Symposium," in Tuana, *Feminist Interpretations of Plato*, pp. 197–215. For another view of Diotima and her role in the *Symposium*, which assumes that it is, in fact, her views that Socrates reports on in this dialogue, see Susan Hawthorne, "Diotima Speaks Through the Body," in Bat-Ami Bar On, ed., *Engendering Origins: Critical Feminist Readings in Plato and Aristotle* (Albany, N.Y.: SUNY Press, 1994), pp. 83–96.

3. As noted above, I use this locution because the conversation on postmodern Jewish philosophy in this dialogue often bleeds into discussions of both "postmodern Judaism" and "Jewish postmodernism."

4. See, especially, Jacques Derrida, "Circumfession," in *Jacques Derrida*, trans. Geoffrey Bennington (Chicago: University of Chicago Press, 1993; originally published in French as *Jacques Derrida* [Paris: Editions du Seuil, 1991]).

5. For example, see Jay Geller, "A Paleontological View of Freud's Study of Religion: Unearthing the *Leitfossil* Circumcision," *Modern Judaism* 13 (1993), pp. 49–70; and Sander Gilman, "The Construction of the Male Jew," in his *Freud, Race, and Gender* (Princeton: Princeton University Press, 1993), pp. 49–92.

6. See, especially, Daniel Boyarin, *Unheroic Conduct: The Rise of Heterosexuality and the Invention of the Jewish Man* (Berkeley: University of California Press, 1997).

7. I thank Richard A. Cohen for sending me a copy of his unpublished essay "Bris Mila, Desire and Levinas," which was presented at the 1996 conference of the Association for Jewish Studies, in Boston. I find Cohen's interpretation of Levinas on circumcision in the main compatible with my own. Cohen, for example, writes: "Rather *bris mila* would be the mark of solidarity, interconnection, the human, insertion in a field of moral forces, of obligations and responsibilities, preceding and exceeding one's animal powers. It would be, as it is, the mark of a *covenant*, where the promise of 'eternity' is used to capture this sense of being bound deeper than a contract which can be kept or broken" (p. 5). Further, in his emphasis on mitzvot as for *both* men and women (pp. 9–10) and on the relation of the involuntary and the "immemorial past" to circumcision as well as "its distance from . . . the individual autonomy" (pp. 1–2), Cohen emphasizes a

reading of Levinas on circumcision that moves toward the inclusion of women in this discourse, even as it makes clear that the bodily subject in question is male. Another important approach to the study of circumcision in these terms is that of Elliot Wolfson, *Through a Speculum That Shines: Vision and Imagination in Medieval Jewish Mysticism* (Princeton: Princeton University Press, 1994). In this and other work, Wolfson demonstrates the phallocentrism of medieval mysticism. In this monumental work, Wolfson's approach to the texts of individual mystics and of the trends in mysticism that they represent is primarily exegetical and explicative, but he does not in any way seek to apologize for or religiously legitimate their phallocentrism. Although he makes abundantly clear that the Shekhinah does not refer to a feminine principle independent of the logic of the masculine in these texts and traditions, Wolfson does not in principle foreclose feminist rereadings of these texts as long as they are based on the recognition that such was not the authorial intent of the medieval mystics.

8. That is, one could more plausibly choose not to live; but choosing to die or to be dead is an epistemologically different matter.

9. There are, of course, instances of adoption of older children in which they might have a say, to a certain extent, in choosing their parents. I am, however, here limiting my reference to the case of "birth parents."

10. See Emmanuel Levinas, *Otherwise Than Being or Beyond Essence*, trans. Alphonso Lingis (The Hague: Martinus Nijhoff Publishers, 1981) and Jean-François Lyotard, *Heidegger and "the Jews,"* trans. Andreas Michel (Minneapolis: University of Minnesota Press, 1990).

11. I do not claim that this covenantal Immemorial is the only way in which the Immemorial is understood by Levinas or others. As the discussion that follows will make clear, there are various ways in which this term has been used and may be understood.

12. See footnote 25 in this section for a reading of the Sinaitic Immemorial that is more historical.

13. See Jean-François Lyotard, *The Postmodern Condition: A Report on Knowledge*, trans. Geoff Bennington and Brian Massumi (Minneapolis: University of Minnesota Press, 1984), p. 81: "*Postmodern* would have to be understood according to the paradox of the future (*post*) anterior (*modo*). . . . It seems to me that the essay (Montaigne) is postmodern, while the fragment (*The Athenaeum*) is modern."

14. See Jean-François Lyotard, *The Differend: Phrases in Dispute* (Minneapolis: University of Minnesota Press, 1988).

15. For some thinkers, the continued existence of the people of Israel and the habitation of the land of Israel constitute two additional traces or signs of covenant.

16. And yet, I think of Tsiporah, who saves her husband, Moses, by circumcising their son. Is this another kind of violence? Is God's wrath toward

Moses a consequence of the latter's failure to "remember" the Immemorial? And why was it a woman after all who had to enact this obligation, making her husband a "bridegroom of blood," after which—like Isaac after the Akedah—Tsiporah virtually disappears from the biblical narrative, except to be gossiped about?

17. See Boyarin, *Unheroic Conduct.*

18. On this trope and its consequences, see, in particular, Elliot Wolfson, *The Circle in the Square* (Albany, N.Y.: SUNY Press, 1996); Howard Eilberg Schwartz, *God's Phallus: And Other Problems for Men and Monotheism* (Boston: Beacon Press, 1994); and Laura Levitt, *Jews and Feminism: The Ambivalent Search for Home* (New York: Routledge Press, 1997).

19. See my "A Matter of Discipline: Reading for Gender in Jewish Philosophy," in Miriam Peskowitz and Laura Levitt, eds., *Judaism Since Gender* (New York: Routledge Press, 1996), pp. 158–173. Also see Elliot Wolfson, *The Circle in the Square.*

20. Jay Geller, "Circumcision and Jewish Women's Identity: Rachel Levin Varnhagen's Failed Assimilation," in Peskowitz and Levitt, eds., *Judaism Since Gender,* pp. 174–187.

21. The naming ceremony, or *Shalom Nekevah,* is not sufficiently analogous. Do Jewish women, then, by virtue of "only" having "circumcision of the heart," approximate or fulfill Paul's vision of true circumcision? No. For while they are not subjected to circumcision, they are required to fulfill the mitzvot. And while Paul polemicizes against literal circumcision of the flesh, he also uses it as a trope to represent the law.

22. It is important to note here that this manner of including Jewish women only addresses those Jews who are religiously oriented and who see themselves as bound by the covenant. It does not resolve the problem of the exclusionary character of this discourse for Jewish or non-Jewish women who do not recognize themselves in these terms. It is possible, however, to interpret the Immemorial in Levinas's thought by emphasizing its atheistic corrective to dogmatism and parochialism rather than in a narrow understanding of the covenant. Still, Levinas's ethics (even in its more atheistic mode) will not be persuasive to all or even to many. So while I am exploring a set of possibilities in Levinas's thought that I think are significant, I do not suggest that this will "solve" all of the problems various feminists have with this matter.

23. Maimonides, for example, treats circumcision as a way of limiting the sex drive, as a mitzvah that—like all of the mitzvot—he understands as having the precise function of disciplining the body. See my "A Matter of Discipline."

24. The problem of "remembering" the Immemorial, and Levinas's approach to it, interestingly resembles Moses Mendelssohn's concern in his *Jerusalem* with the problem of language necessarily introducing idolatrous

misunderstandings of God. Mendelssohn imagines that ancient Judaism offered a way of preserving and passing on to the next generation a non-idolatrous understanding of God by a form of learning from communal practice. This practice of learning would begin with the son asking the father or teacher why he is doing what he is doing. This beginning with practice was supposed to serve as a corrective to the ultimately idolatrous character of language (i.e., thought or text) preceding doing. Idolatry, however, was a problem in ancient Israel, and as Mendelssohn notes, as early as the time of Samuel the Mosaic Constitution had begun to "fissure." Still, he seems to offer this iconoclastic capacity of Judaism as an important, if fallible, resource. (See, especially, Mendelssohn, *Jerusalem*, trans. Alan Arkush [Hanover, N.H.: University Press of New England & Brandeis University, 1983], pp. 103–106, 128, 132.) Both this iconoclasm and the "remembering" of the Immemorial are in different ways both impossible and necessary. Both are, furthermore, tied to "doing before understanding" and to an understanding of the "Greek," or "Eternal Truths," as in need of supplemental iconoclastic critique by the "Hebrew," or the "Ceremonial Law." Might one even suggest that Mendelssohn, like Levinas, is concerned in *Jerusalem* with preserving an idea of the divine as infinite? I cannot delve further into this question here.

25. It is important to note, however, the tradition that all the souls of future Jewish generations were present at Sinai to receive the commandments and to contract the covenant. This would yield another reading of the immemorial obligation such that it would be a remembrance of a historical event, thus no longer giving the Immemorial its peculiar transcendental character, as found in both the thought of Levinas and Lyotard. Indeed, the term *Immemorial* would no longer be appropriate on this reading. Alternatively, one might refer to the immemorial moment or dimension of the memory of a historical event, be that Sinai or the Shoah. In such a reframing, the Sinaitic covenantal Immemorial approximates that of the Shoah in its temporal structure. Would not, then, any and every event also be immemorial in this sense? This is the point that Derrida makes when he says, "And I will not speak here of the *holocaust*, except to say this: there is the date of a certain holocaust the hell of our memory, but there is a holocaust for every date, somewhere in the world at every hour. Every hour is unique, whether it comes back or whether, the last, it comes no more, no more than the sister, the same, its other *revenant*, coming back." See Jacques Derrida, "Shibboleth," *Midrash and Literature*, trans. Joshua Wilner, eds. Geoffrey H. Hartmen and Sanford Budick (New Haven: Yale University Press, 1986), p. 336. While Lyotard seems to conflate the transcendental and historical Immemorials, it is the transcendental Immemorial that is configured through the discourse of the historical Immemorial. For a more detailed treatment of Lyotard on the Immemorial, see my "Ecri-

ture Judaïque: Where Are the Jews in Western Discourse?" in Angelika Bammer, *Displacements: Cultural Identities in Question* (Bloomington: Indiana University Press, 1994), pp. 182–201. See also the next section, "Thinking About the Holocaust," for a further discussion of these issues.

26. See my "Failing Speech: Post-Holocaust Writing and the Discourse of Postmodernism," *Semeia* 40, 1987.

27. This is especially so with regard to the writings of Derrida, Maurice Blanchot, Edmond Jabes, and Jean-François Lyotard (see my "Failing Speech" and "Ecriture Judaïque").

28. My analysis and discussion of these terms in this response is necessarily brief, and thus, incomplete.

29. It is important here to note that what Levinas calls the "face" of the other person should not be taken literally. The word "face" refers to speech, to the discourse of the other person. He is careful to note that if one notices or focuses on details such as the color of the other person's eyes, then one is not "seeing" their face. However, it is important that Levinas chooses the word "face" to signify the otherness of the other person. Some commentators have chastised those interpreters of Levinas who reify the "face" as the literal face. But, surely, it is not insignificant that this term is used. I do not suggest that one interpret the term literally, but rather, that one regard the face of the other person as distinctive, as not my own. Just as the nonliteral reading of the face as discourse critiques a potentially idolatrous relation or investment, so does the recognition of the face of the other person as other—that is, as not my own—enable a critique of an idolatrous return to the same—that is, in seeing the other person as another me. Although "face" must, therefore, not be taken literally, neither should it be considered simply replaceable by other, more abstract and nonbodily terms. For there are two kinds of idolatrous (and hence, unethical) relation critiqued in Levinas's use of the word "face."

30. Indeed, Levinas does not use the term *Immemorial* to refer to the Shoah. Lyotard, on the other hand, as I have already noted, problematically identifies the two: the Holocaust and the transcendental (perhaps for Lyotard, the better term would be the "always already primordial") Immemorial. I am trying here, as I have indicated, to distinguish between these two Immemorials, the better to raise the question of their possible critical relation.

31. See Levitt, *Jews and Feminism*, for an extended inquiry into the problematics of "home" in Judaism and feminism as well as in their intersection.

32. I include here the formation of Jewish Orthodoxy as in part a defensive response to modernity.

6

Listening to Speak:
A Response to Dialogues in
Postmodern Jewish Philosophy

Elliot R. Wolfson

The Text of Suffering

The task set before me is to respond to the Dialogues in Postmodern Jewish Philosophy recorded in this volume. In order to fulfill this task, I am called upon to be a listener. My role as listener is predicated on the fact that I did not participate in the actual dialogue. Indeed, my listening is belated, as I have come to hear after the words have been spoken. But in the listening I am engaged as one who speaks. My hearing is itself a manner of speaking, for the text of the dialogue not only preserves the discussions of the participants but opens up those discussions for all readers who listen to the voices echoing in the traces of the text. The hearing that is a form of dialogic speech may be likened to the receiving of a gift, which as Ochs reminds us, is an act of faith rather than hope. The very project of postmodern Jewish philosophy must ensue from this act of faith, which takes shape "in response to gifts received directly from an other, rather than in re-sponse to promises" (p. 56). There is no promise conveyed here, only a gift bestowed upon the reader. A gift that is pleasurable to receive but also painful to bear: the gift of faith without hope.

A keen awareness runs throughout these conversations that post-modern Jewish philosophy originates in the dialogic recognition of suffering. The point is stated emphatically by Gibbs: "Suffering has pride of place in postmodern Jewish philosophy, more than hope, well-being, or any eudaemonia, more than even knowledge" (p. 46). The failure of modernism is related to its inattentiveness to suffering. Ochs says: "Philosophy is postmodern when its criticism is aimed at repairing. The modern situation needs critique because of suffering. Modern philosophy assumes a privileged status without taking note of suffering" (p. 12). The suffering is felt on many levels—the suffering of the self, the suffering of the other, the suffering of Israel, the suffering of God, the suffering of being. To be is to suffer, to sense one's otherness, one's belatedness, the fate of the listener who has not had a chance to speak. The experience of suffering is exacerbated by the fact that the postmodern sensibility emerges from a tear in the texture of tradition, a rupture with the historical past—from the conviction that ultimate truth is not ultimately attainable, and the acceptance that all knowledge is conditional, relative, and partial. The indeterminacy of meaning is the quintessential sign of the postmodernist rejection of essentialism and the concomitant awareness that the light of truth is refracted through a prism of multiple perspectives. Like other varieties of postmodernism, a postmodern Jewish philosophy must embrace epistemological suspicion regarding all totalizing and dichotomizing forms of knowledge and praxis.

For postmodern Jewish philosophy, moreover, the distrust of universalist and essentialist claims is intensified by the memory of the Holocaust. I agree with Kepnes, therefore, when he asserts that after the Holocaust "there is a rethinking of modern Judaism that is part of the rethinking I associate with postmodern Jewish thinking. . . . '[P]ost-Holocaust' is one of the markers of the new beginning that is postmodern Jewish thinking" (p. 42). But the philosophical significance of the Holocaust clearly extends beyond the parameters of the Jewish community. Humanity at large, and not merely the Jews, must be challenged by the convergence of the nihilistic disregard for all moral truth, on the one hand, and the totalitarian claim to absolute political truth, on the other. The postmodern consciousness is suspended between the poles of anarchy and tyranny—and therein lies its suffering. Ochs aptly describes the "narrative of suffering" that informs the postmodern epistemology: "But now, after modernity, we know that we cannot prove anything universally except that wherever anyone claims there is suffering—wherever we see someone in pain—suffering is there. Marks of suffering, therefore, enable us to begin conversations across community borders—not to complete them, but to begin" (p. 56).

By acknowledging suffering, the postmodern project attempts to alleviate it. "The wake-up call that alerts us to suffering," says Gibbs, "also commands us to remedy the suffering" (p. 47). The call to suffering is the very nature of divine revelation, which Gibbs characterizes (following Rosenzweig) as an interruption: "Revelation is a two-party relation, requiring interpretation by the human who receives it. The core is the interruption of my world, the breaking-in upon me, which alerts me to others' suffering, others' needs" (p. 49). For Jews (and certainly others) who live in the post-Holocaust world, the alleviation of pain is predicated not on forgetting the perpetrators of the obscene and violent crimes against humanity but on extending the dialogic relationship to embrace even the enemy. "What binds us to each other," Gibbs reminds his partners in conversation, "is that each is liable for the other—and that is a way of seeing the responsibility to protect the other's integrity" (p. 46). Postmodernism fosters an inclusive dialogue that excludes none but those who would exclude the other.

In the postmodern world, the certitude of hegemony has given way to the ambivalence of doubt, and doubt is precisely the epistemic condition that secures the ethical right of the other to voice an opinion. Quoting Ochs again, "Postmodernity is not a new way to delimit our own discursive freedom but a chance finally to speak" (p. 43). Gibbs, too, refers to this task, but he formulates it specifically in terms of Judaism: "This Jewish tradition of reading and writing, of texts and libraries, serves as our companion for addressing the suffering of our age, the failure of historical progress, and the freedom of others. . . . Jewish textuality is at core a way of heeding other voices" (pp. 22–23).

When the listener is allowed to speak, philosophical discourse is transformed into a mode of rectification, "reforming modernism" rather than "replacing it with something altogether new" (p. 39). Relating this activity of reform more generally to rabbinic hermeneutics, Gibbs notes: "The rabbinic reader's task is repentance, *teshuvah*. For postmodernists, this means turning back to traditions of practice from which modernity has cut itself off" (p. 38). Rendering this hermeneutical act of return in psychoanalytical terms, Kepnes contrasts the approach of modernism with that of postmodernism: The modernist orientation is to "overthrow an offending tradition or practice as if it were the oedipal father," whereas the "postmodern model is one of dialogic reintegration with the father" (p. 39). Building on this (admittedly androcentric) analogy, Gibbs comments that the re-membering of the father on the part of the son is an act of repentance for both father and son. Jewish postmodernism, therefore, has two distinguishing marks: an emphasis on continuity with modernity and an acknowledgment of one's own sins through the study of the past. Summing up the main point of this discussion, Ochs notes that Jewish postmodernism is a form of *teshuvah*, "reforming modernity, not abandoning it" (p. 39).

The traditional category of *teshuvah*—literally, "return"—is certainly an apt term to convey the implicit ethical task of postmodern philosophical engagement. However, I would introduce as well the more technical kabbalistic idea of *tikkun*, restoration or repair. In the final analysis, the two terms convey the same idea, for the return is a form of repair and the repair a form of return, a homecoming that restores an originary sense of balance, harmony, and belonging. Indeed, Kepnes himself in one place expresses this very insight when he notes that "postmodern Judaism is a repair, a return, a rehabilitation" (p. 25). Similarly, Gibbs remarks that postmodern Jewish philosophy can be seen as a means to rectify "modernity's broken relationship with traditional texts" (p. 50). The moderns are portrayed by Gibbs typologically (rather than historically) as "one-dimensional prophets" who "see only what is oppressing them in the tradition" (p. 47). This inability of the modernist orientation to retrieve anything positive from the tradition is emphasized as well by Ochs when he remarks: "The modernist's complaint is a reliable sign that something has gone wrong, but it fails to tell us precisely what and where the problem was and is. It is in that sense a doubly negative revelation: It negates something, and it fails to provide positive information about what that something is" (p. 48). The primary focal point of the *tikkun* of Jewish postmodernism is textual, a return to the traditional text. In Ochs's words, "Modernity's complaints are merely negative revelations, but postmodernity's corrections are a way of rereading those revelations in the light of traditional discourse" (p. 49).

The Suffering of the Text

The participants in the dialogue all basically agree that Jewish postmodernism is distinguished from other forms of postmodernism on account of the rich literary legacy of Judaism. Postmodern Jewish philosophy does not advocate the return to any text for the sake of textual grounding, but the return to Jewish texts with the hope of rectifying the breach in traditional practice and belief brought about by the modernist project of subordinating revelation to reason. The linguistic, cultural, and religious practices distinctive to the Jewish community, Ochs writes, "are not organized around first principles per se, but around certain primary texts and text traditions." He continues: "Our postmodern philosophy emerges as a way of reading these texts, participating in these streams, and thereby identifying, in context-specific ways, the first principles for conducting context-specific tasks of reasoning. . . . Rather than placing rationality over and against textuality as a competing or prior practice, we may redescribe rationality as both servant and consort of the text" (p. 20). Kepnes relates this feature of postmodern Jewish philosophy to the conjunction of Jewish subjectivity and Jewish textuality: "Thus postmodern Jewish subjectivity is an interpersonal and communal task requiring constant interaction with Jewish texts" (p. 24). In an obvious turn away from the universalizing tendency of modern philosophical approaches to scriptural revelation, Kepnes asserts: "Jewish postmoderns also have recourse to positive revelation—understood not as a universal revelation of truth, but as the Word such as it was received by our particular, finite tradition and community of discourse. If we take a hint from Rosenzweig and begin with love—or as I see it, with the positive Jewish revelation of the Torah—we begin not only with resources of hope and faith that replenish our souls but also with strategies of community, jurisprudence, and pedagogy to face suffering—strategies that the deconstructive postmodern philosophers lack" (p. 58). Kepnes focuses on the specificity of the Jewish tradition and thus he distinguishes the Jewish postmoderns from postmodern adherents to deconstructionism: Only the former have the means to confront suffering in a constructive way.

In a similar vein, Ochs contrasts postmodernists influenced by Derrida, who "know only the modern context of interrupted discourses," with Jewish postmodernists, who "retain their 'traditional' texts as contexts for rebuilding traditional discourses, rather than merely deconstructing them." He goes on to say: "The advantage of Jewish (and in this sense, also of Christian) postmodernism is that its texts provide a prototype of the infinite author of deconstruction as well as of the creator" (p. 51). Scripture thus presents the model for "infinite deconstruction," which is the corrective to a more Hellenic postmodern hermeneutics. The text of Scripture provides the prototype of one who simultaneously destroys and creates. Here Ochs has hit upon a foundational point in rabbinic thinking, expressed both in midrashic and kabbalistic texts: God both creates and destroys; indeed, he destroys by creating and he creates by destroying. In standard accounts of divine creativity in classical and medieval Jewish sources, too much emphasis has been placed on God's exclusive role as creator and far less attention has been given to God's destructive side, which is in fact an intrinsic aspect of the creative process. Consider the comment attributed to R. Abbahu on the verse "There was evening and there was morning, the first day" (Gen. 1:5): "From here [we learn that] the Holy One, blessed be He, created worlds and destroyed them, until He created these. He said: These give me pleasure, but those did not give me pleasure" (*Genesis Rabbah* 3:7). Bracketing the historicist question concerning the ideational background of this passage and focusing on its philosophic import, we can say that the rabbinic voice behind this text wished to communicate the idea that God creates by destroying. That the element of deconstruction is critical to divine creation is also attested in the rabbinic notion that God created the world by joining together the attributes of mercy and judgment, which are correlated respectively to the names YHWH and Elohim. According to one midrashic parable, this may be compared to a king who had two empty cups; if he placed hot water in them, they would crack, but if he placed cold water in them, they would freeze. Hence, he mixed the two together so that they could exist. Similarly, God calculated that if he created the word solely through the attribute of mercy, the sins of humanity would multiply, but if he created it through the attribute of judgment, the world could not exist. By mixing the two attributes together, however, he could create and sustain the world (*Genesis Rabbah* 12:15). The attribute of judgment is not identified explicitly as the destructive force of God, but such an identification is clearly implied. Only the amelioration of judgment by mercy prevents God's judgmental side from destroying the world. Creation occurs through the admixture of mercy and judgment, the creative and destructive powers of the divine.

The full implications of these ideas are drawn out in the medieval kabbalistic sources. According to a bold idea expressed in the *Zohar* and further developed in the Lurianic material of the sixteenth century, the first act of divine creativity involves the elimination of the forces of impurity from the Godhead. This act of catharsis of evil is related to the attribute of judgment or divine limitation, which is referred to in the Lurianic kabbalah by the technical term *tsimtsum* (withdrawal). In his own midrashic interpretation, Ochs depicts the destruction of the infinite, or the process whereby the infinite gives itself up, as a quality of God's attribute of mercy (p. 57). In the relevant kabbalistic sources, by contrast, it is clearly the attribute of judgment by means of which the infinite delimits itself. The creative process necessitates the negation of the infinite. The kabbalists well perceived that creation is dependent on delimitation. Expansion and contraction, egression and regression, are not mutually exclusive antinomies. Disclosure is a form of concealment, just as concealment is a form of disclosure. Translated grammatologically, this dialectic signifies that every affirmation is a negation and every negation an affirmation. The finitude of temporality, which is correlated with the theological category of creation, signifies a sense of dying on the part of God. From this perspective we can speak of divine suffering at the very core of existence. If God did not suffer his own death as the infinite, there would be no existence outside of the infinite God. In line with the position adopted by Ochs, one can say that for the kabbalists, the act of healing, which I assume implies the process of making whole, can be attributed to the infinite only when the infinite is itself destroyed as infinite—in other words, when the infinite becomes finite.

The primordial delimitation of the infinite can be expressed also in terms of the textualization of God—that is, God's becoming concretely manifest in the form of the Torah. One of the basic insights of the kabbalistic tradition, or what may be called a ground concept, is the incarnational theology of the Torah as the garment in which the trace of the divine light is constricted. The concretization and delimitation of the infinite in the body of the Torah is expressed also in terms of the identification of God and His name, on the one hand, and the identification of the name and the Torah, on the other. God's donning the garment of the name, which is the Torah, is an act of self-constriction suffered by the divine for the sake of creation. The Torah, therefore, is not only a text that "suffers our reading and our not reading," as Ochs put it (p. 58), but it is a text that arises from God's own suffering. The hermeneutical task of reading, which is affirmed over and over again in this dialogue as the central concern of postmodern Jewish philosophy, is a form of participating in the suffering of God.

In one passage, Ochs comments that for Jews, "circumcision, as opposed to castration, signifies a hermeneutic that preserves the text—or tradition or impulse—while delimiting its potential oppressiveness" (p. 37). Reflecting on this incisive remark, let me first note that I am not certain that we can speak of circumcision as a hermeneutic that delimits the text's potential oppressiveness. On the contrary, it is conceivable that a feminist reader would find the trope of circumcision rather oppressive and exclusionary. In a similar vein, the Pauline reading of circumcision, which must be seen as inner development of the Pharisaic midrashic tradition, underscores the restrictive nature of circumcision. The potentially oppressive consequences of the correlation of circumcision with the study of the Torah are made explicit in kabbalistic sources according to which both gentiles and women are excluded from this fundamental rite. The kabbalists express this exclusion, further, in terms of a structural homology between the covenant of the foreskin and the covenant of the tongue, which was first established in *Sefer Yetsirah*. A typical expression of this homology is found in the following words of the thirteenth-century Spanish kabbalist, Joseph Gikatilla: "If Israel had not received the covenant of the flesh, they would never have merited the Torah, which is the covenant of the tongue.... Therefore the Torah is only given to one who has received the covenant of the flesh, and from the covenant of the flesh one enters into the covenant of the tongue, which is the reading of the Torah" (*Sha'arei 'Orah*, ed. J. Ben-Shlomo [Jerusalem, 1981], 1:115). One would be hard pressed to deny the oppressiveness that emerges from the nexus of circumcision and Torah study as it has taken shape within the matrix of Jewish esotericism.

There is no question, however, that the analogy that Ochs draws between circumcision and hermeneutics resonates deeply with the rabbinic tradition. Expanding on his comments, I would emphasize that circumcision as a trope for the hermeneutical process underscores the painfulness of reading, a painfulness that relates to the opening of the flesh that both marks and seals the covenantal relationship between God and Israel. Divine writing and human reading share in the suffering of the text.

But what does it mean to suffer as a reader, to read as one who suffers? Just as God suffers in delimiting himself by donning the garment of the Torah, so the reader must constrict his or her interpretation to be cloaked by the text. A characteristic feature of postmodern hermeneutics, as I have already emphasized, is the acceptance of the indeterminacy of meaning. To an extent, as Kepnes himself asserts (p. 58), the rabbinic hermeneutic anticipates the postmodernist perspective by positing multiple meanings (represented by the symbol of seventy faces) to every scriptural verse. However, this does not imply that there is no meaning intrinsic to the text. The complex interplay of text and reader requires the recognition of the mutual relationship between the two that precludes complete identification or diametric opposition. The text is not simply what the reader says, nor is the reader merely reflecting what the text says. Interpretation arises from the confrontation of text and reader, which results in the concomitant bestowal and elicitation of meaning. The reader, therefore, must limit the range of possible meanings by learning how to decode the footprints that the author left behind in the text. In this sense, the hermeneutical process can be viewed as an emulation of the suffering of God that results in the constriction of the divine light into the form of the letters of the Torah. Reading, therefore, is a reenactment of circumcision, an act of de-cision that binds the male Jew into a covenantal relationship with the God of Israel.

This aspect of reading as suffering relates, moreover, to the erotic quality of textual study to which Kepnes periodically refers (pp. 58, 60). The joyfulness of study is indeed related to the eros for God experienced through engagement with the text. I would not, however, dichotomize eros and suffering. On the contrary, the erotic involves a subtle dialectic of pleasure and pain, satisfaction and denial. The eros of reading necessitates the suffering of the reader as he/she confronts the otherness of the text in its inherent resistance.

Suffering Textually for the Text of Suffering

The participants in these extraordinary conversations convey a unique sense of Jewish postmodernism and its return to the text. The postmodern turning back to Jewish textuality is a corrective to the modernist turning away from Judaism, the "repression of the Jewish for the sake of the modern," the abandonment of "Jewish particularity for the sake of the abstract universal" (p. 25). Kepnes expresses a shared sentiment of the group when he asserts that "Jewish postmodernists try to recover a relationship to the particularistic forms of thinking, interpreting, and living that we associate with Jewish tradition" (p. 35). If the fallacy of modernism lay in its universalizing approach to revelation and in its consequent tendency to ignore the contextual nature of specific traditions, the risk of postmodernism is a potential emphasis on the particularity of a tradition to the exclusion of others. Here, in some measure, I am reiterating a dualistic logic that imposes a false dichotomy upon the postmodern sensibility. Gibbs anticipates my concern when he comments that on the one hand, postmodern Jewish philosophy is not exclusively Jewish, for it does not in principle exclude anyone, but on the other, it does appear in a particularly Jewish context. "Thus its particularity must not be seen as dyadically paired with universality—as though if it is Jewish, then it is not universal, and if universal, then not Jewish" (p. 22). I appreciate this attempt to avoid the extremes of dogmatic particularism (the Jew experiences some truth uniquely) and apologetic universalism (what is true in the Jewish tradition is shared universally by all human cultures). Moreover, I endorse Gibbs's observation that the hallmark of the logic of postmodern Jewish philosophy will be a "logic that can open to generality without dissolving particularity" (p. 23). Similarly, Kepnes emphasizes that "postmodern Jews do not return to a ghettoized Judaism isolated from other cultures and faiths but to a Judaism set in the context of cultural and religious pluralism" (p. 25). For his part, Ochs also demonstrates concern with narrow-mindedness when he cautions against a tendency of Holocaust theology to focus exclusively on the suffering of the Jews. To learn about human suffering, one must also read the suffering of other people (p. 42).

In spite of these well-intentioned qualifications, one cannot help but come away from reading this document with the feeling that there is a real potential in the postmodern Jewish project for a lapse into an ethnocentrism that could promote rather than heal the suffering of others. It is telling that in response to a question of Kepnes regarding the hermeneutical privileging of suffering over the joy of study, Ochs responded that suffering begins a conversation across community borders, whereas joy is limited to the community itself (pp. 55–56). Why can suffering be shared but joy cannot? I do not know the answer to this question, but at the very least one must be concerned about a hermeneutical ideal that excludes the possibility of sharing the joy of studying Jewish texts with non-Jews. Kepnes is quite emphatic about this point when he describes the study of Torah as a "liturgical performance." When asked by Ochs if this is an activity that is limited to a particular community, Kepnes responds:

"I think so. . . . The liturgical dimension requires Jewish texts, the Torah. And that means it also requires Jewish readers" (pp. 60–61). Gibbs is quick to challenge this parochialism: "Jewish texts also can speak to non-Jews, if they want to listen. Non-Jews can experience what you are calling the liturgical dimension of reading together." Significantly, Ochs responds to this remark by adding that non-Jews can participate in the liturgical experience of reading Jewish texts only "as anthropologists." At an earlier point in the dialogue, Ochs remarks that non-Jews engaged in the relation of Jewish philosophy to postmodernity "are writing about the intellectual part," and they leave out the "Jewish praxis" (p. 12). It is the latter, however, that truly defines postmodern Jewish philosophers. "Non-Jews who do postmodern Jewish philosophy do other things, very important things, but not exactly what we do" (p. 12).

In my opinion, this discussion touches on the most important ethical issue to emerge from these thoughtful and insightful conversations regarding the nature of a postmodern Jewish philosophy. The participants themselves are clearly not all in agreement on this foundational point. I would hope, however, that as this project becomes more refined, careful attention will be paid to this volatile issue. Without denying the obvious need to affirm the particularity of Jewish textuality as the central concern for postmodern Jewish philosophers, it is equally important to understand that the texts that make up the tradition reflect a constant and dialectical interplay between the internal Jewish axis and the external axis of other cultures. To emphasize a Jewish particularism isolated from the larger cultural matrix in which it takes shape may result in the reification of the ethnocentric elements of traditional texts. And let us admit forthrightly that in traditional Jewish sources there have been expressions of cultural elitism that on occasion have bordered on racial discrimination. Under the proper political conditions, such an attitude might generate or justify the enslavement and degradation of the other on the part of Jews. The consequence of a hermeneutical turn that overemphasizes the particularity of the Jewish reader may be the augmentation of suffering in the world rather than a greater sensitivity to suffering, which has been upheld as the critical role of postmodern Jewish philosophy. The postmodern study of Jewish texts must be predicated on a critical assessment of the tradition in all of its multivocality. Ochs is correct when he asserts that "tradition" represents "those collections of texts that bear meaning and require critical inquiry" (p. 32). The key here is the emphasis placed on critical inquiry, which involves confronting the good and the bad in the traditional texts with openness of mind and integrity of spirit. Only by interacting with the tradition in this decidedly nonapologetic manner will the danger of lapsing into an ethnocentrism marked by an indifference to the suffering of the other be curtailed.

The challenge for postmodern Jewish philosophy is to facilitate the growth of a culture based on the textual specificity of the past without losing sight of the place that Judaism must occupy in the human community at large. We must get beyond the dichotomy of the universal and the particular, but not by reducing the one to the other. On the contrary, the particularity of the Jewish tradition is meaningful only to the extent that it improves on the moral condition of humanity. To achieve that goal, it is necessary to examine the traditional sources with a critical sensibility and a willingness to modify aspects of the tradition that augment the suffering in the world. From that perspective we can speak of the postmodern philosophical enterprise as suffering textually for the sake of the text of suffering. As a people that embodies the suffering of the text in the text of their suffering, the Jews have a distinctive role to play in this process.

7

Joining the Narrators:
A Philosophy of
Talmudic Hermeneutics

Almut Sh. Bruckstein

What Is the Postmodern Jewish Project?

Commentary often is offered as a spontaneous and oral response to a classical or traditional script.[1] Such a commentary then may or may not be put into the various forms of written glosses. In the current project, matters are reversed: The oral, spontaneous narrative, the "Initial Conversation"—involuntarily garbed as "script"—provides the groundwork for the written commentary. Written commentary carried out by a single author, even by one who has been an active participant in the initial conversation, exhibits features of systematization, definition, and critical judgment—that is, it is characterized by the kind of unambiguity that distinguishes the written word from the multifaceted spontaneity of oral interaction. The chapter entitled "Monologic Definitions" thus constitutes the only written, monologic layer of the "conversational philosophical project" before us.

Individual evaluation and written commentary, in turn, may ignite another spark of oral discourse, creating a "new" narrative interacting with the "initial" one—mediating and elevating the original transcript by eliciting from it a significance not yet explored. The transcript of such a "narrative on a narrative" constitutes a central part of the original project, the chapter entitled "Dialogic Practices." The trialogue of voices there preserves the immediacy of oral

> The Talmud preserves the openness and the challenge of living speech. It cannot be summarized by the term "dialogue" which is so abused today.
> Emmanuel Levinas,
> *Nine Talmudic Readings* [1]

105

discourse documented in the unmediated form of the spoken word. The pluralist principle of "polyphony" is then fully affirmed by the postmodern Jewish philosophy group's inviting other voices to join in this discourse—voices like my own and that of the reader, whose freedom to dissent is protected by the postmodern project. In defiance of the principle of identity, the pluralist principle affirms the "alterity of the other"; and in defiance of the principle of totality, it affirms the particularity of the "single voice." Thus, it renounces the striving for a "harmonious whole" at all costs, discarding it as totalitarian uniformity, a strategy of violence inherent in the great systems of the late nineteenth century.

> True polyphony means radical independence of the respective voices; . . . dissonance represents all that is pious and spiritual, whereas harmony stands for the enticement of hell, i.e., it is reserved for the sphere of banality and of the commonplace.
> Thomas Mann,
> *Doktor Faustus*   [2]

The underlying theme of the entire project is the question of "Talmudic hermeneutics"—also referred to as "oral tradition"—which has been characteristic of Jewish tradition ever since Moses is reported to have received an oral teaching from God. The Jewish Sages refer to this "original oral teaching" as a *mysterium*, a "private teaching" meant initially for Moses alone. Moses, however, decides to share his *megillat setarim*, his "private notebook," with all of Israel and ultimately with all of the world. The initial oral teaching—which Moses shared in an act of personal generosity—provides the basis not only for the so-called "written Torah" but also for the entire organism that we call our "oral tradition," including Midrash, Mishnah, and Talmud.

> The Torah was a personal gift for Moses and his descendants, as it says: "Write down for yourself . . ."(Exod. 34:27). Moses, however, showed generosity by sharing his gift with all Israel.
> *Talmud Bavli* [Babylonian Talmud, hereafter TB], *Nedarim* 38a

These, in turn, give rise to an uncountable number of "written" commentaries evoked by the discussions of the Jewish Sages. Traditionally speaking, oral discourse precedes written commentary.

When Jewish thinkers today set out to define themselves in terms of "postmodern identity," they do so by reenacting the Talmudic model of "living speech," giving priority to the oral tradition with its emphasis on the inexhaustible meaning of texts and its respect for and sensitivity to the minority opinion. Thus the Jewish "oral tradition" is committed to an un-

> Why do we record the minority opinions along with the majority decisions? For when a court in the future weighs

compromising ideal of justice
that may be understood as the
protection of the voice that differs. However, in contemporary

them anew, it may be inclined to accept
them.

Mishnah Eduyot 1:5

rabbinic Talmudic discourse, the principle of nurturing "the voice
that differs" seems to have faded from the agenda. "Postmodern
Jewish philosophy" thus envisions the advancement of a *post-
Talmudic* culture committed to the task of deconstructing and
reevaluating the Talmudic model in order to affirm its "polyphony"—defined as the protection of particularity from the violent
power of any one-dimensional system.

I would like the reader to note that the preoccupation of postmodern Jewish thinkers with methodological issues by no means reflects an abstract interest in questions of hermeneutics. To the contrary, their commitment to the openness and spontaneity of oral
discourse, as well as their concern for the dissident voice and its protection, translates directly into an active and unambiguous position
on such concrete matters as violence and suffering, totalitarian
power and political tolerance, dogma and the freedom of thought
and speech, pluralism and nonviolence, and so on. When Robert
Gibbs, Peter Ochs, and Steven Kepnes in "Dialogic Practices" touch
upon subjects such as *teshuvah* and tradition, suffering and the
Shoah, the other's freedom, "negative theology," and the "face of
the other," their commitment to an open mode of discourse has immediate bearing upon their judgment concerning the philosophical,
historical, and traditional issues involved. Each cultural history and
each religious tradition is thus prone to be a product of a certain
kind of hermeneutics: "Interpretation" is the construction of history.

Continental Links to the American Debate

In May 1996, I had the privilege of attending an international conference on Hermann Cohen's philosophy of religion in Jerusalem.
Hermann Cohen, the most critical of modern Jewish philosophers,
a reformer of Kantian philosophy and a master of Jewish sources,
dedicated his late work to constructing a "Religion of Reason out
of the Sources of Judaism." One of the dominant themes of this conference was the question of whether there is a cogent connection between Hermann Cohen's earlier critical, secular philosophy—in
other words, his "logic"[2] and his "ethics"[3]—and his Jewish work.

Cohen himself claims that there is, in fact, an intimate correlation between his own secular philosophical method and the content of the traditional Jewish sources.

Here I wish to explicate three features of this relationship that have an intimate bearing on our postmodern discussion of Talmudic modes of discourse: (1) Cohen's secular philosophy is concerned primarily with the development of an innovative, critical method of interpretative thinking. (2) The classical rabbinic sources, in their "oral tradition," exhibit a unique way of interpreting and reading texts. (3) There is an intimate correlation between the two—that is, between the Jewish "oral tradition" and Cohen's own philosophical method.[4] More specifically, Cohen's philosophical method might even be predicated upon the methods of interpretation and modes of discourse that characterize Jewish tradition.

If my reading of Cohen is accurate, we have found a philosophical agenda that correlates with "Jewish tradition" in such a way that it (a) provides us with a conceptual tool to "define" what we mean by "post-Talmudic" discourse, and (b) enables us to remain critical in our appreciation of the "oral tradition," distinguishing hermeneutical strategies of openness from those of dogmatism. Dogma, according to Cohen, is a genuinely "un-Jewish" phenomenon in that its ultimate fixation of meaning violates the infinite "origin-ality" of the Jewish texts.

The Cohenian teaching concerning a "Jewish hermeneutics of origin" made its way into Rosenzweig's *The Star of Redemption*,[5] where Rosenzweig modified it ingeniously. When American postmodern Jewish philosophers make reference to a philosophical critique of totality in terms of infinity (or a critique of identity in terms of alterity), they speak a vaguely defined language that is based primarily on the philosophical teachings of Emmanuel Levinas. Thus, postmodern Jewish philosophy is linked to a debate within continental philosophy whose roots are nowhere explicit in the discussion. Reading through "Dialogic Practices," I appreciated Robert Gibbs's consistent attempts to ground the discussion in Rosenzweig's *Sprachdenken* as well as in Levinas's *Totality and Infinity*.[6] But I missed the additional inspiration that the discussion could have gained had it made reference to Cohen's philosophy of creative thinking; his ethics of justice, primarily concerned with the suffering of human beings; and his theory concerning the primacy of oral tradition. According to Cohen, Judaism acts out these ideal premises in an exemplary manner.

In the following narrative, I link two discourses that were heretofore held separate, envisioning their creative interaction—namely, our discussion of post-Talmudic modes of discourse, which makes reference to the work of Levinas and Rosenzweig, and the European neo-Kantian discussion of Cohen's philosophical work. Until recently, German academic discourse on neo-Kantian philosophy in general, and on the philosophy of Hermann Cohen in particular, has been largely confined to historical discussion. Today there is a profound awareness among European scholars of the contemporary social, political, and hermeneutical significance of Cohen's thought.[7] A realization of the importance of Jewish studies for a full appreciation of Cohen's work is still wanting. For our purpose here, however, the European discussion of Cohen's general philosophy may prove helpful in establishing a *philosophical* hermeneutical agenda for the American debate on postmodernity that can account for the specificity and uniqueness of "Talmudic discourse" without ceding the discussion to any of the postmodern prejudices against "modern philosophy." For postmodern thinkers generally, the terms *modern* and *philosophical* are loaded with emotional negativity, whereas the "positivity" of such vaguely defined terms as *postmodern* and *Talmudic* are postulated with rather dogmatic presumptuousness. This dogmatic impasse—characteristic of the entire postmodern discussion—seems unavoidable in a discourse that declares the impotence of philosophy, denigrating its "logocentricity," and thus dispensing with its power of criticism. If we link our discussion, in contrast, to a philosophical mode of discourse defined both in terms of spontaneous creativity and in terms of critical judgment, we may retain the originality of the "oral tradition," of Rosenzweig's *Sprachdenken*, while at the same time retrieving the critical function of "philosophy" without which our definition of "post-Talmudic discourse" shall have no safeguard against dogmatism. Following in the revolutionary spirit of Cohen and his mistrust of any truth-claims brought forward in the name of "history," one might well dispense with the terms *postmodern* and *modern*. In the context of a discourse whose emphasis on the primacy of interpretation implicitly rejects any historicist thinking, such terms seem counterproductive.

Cohen's Logic and His Concept of "Oral Tradition"

How do we, then, provide guidance for post-Talmudic modes of discourse that preserve the critical function of philosophical judgment at the same time as we advocate the specificity of Jewish "oral tradition" and its ways of reading and interpretation?

Rosenzweig made an interesting comment about reading books in general and philosophical and Jewish books in particular, signifying the kind of "logic of origin" that I wish to pursue here and that I think indicates one of the hermeneutical principles of "oral tradition." The remark is found in Rosenzweig's much-cited "New Thinking" of 1925, advising the perplexed reader of *The Star of Redemption* to read the book from its end to its beginning, and claiming that in a philosophical book of any significance, every sentence originates in the one

> In this order the conclusion is not derived from the preceding but from the following sentence.
>
> Franz Rosenzweig, *Das neue Denken* [3]

following it, and not—as the uninitiated might assume—in the one preceding it.

Let me therefore begin with a commentary on the conclusion of "Dialogic Practices." There the participants invoke the midrashic story of Moses ascending on high, asking God to show him Rabbi Akiva, who in the future, many generations later, would interpret each letter of the Torah stroke by stroke. Having been granted his request, Moses finds himself in the classroom of Rabbi Akiva—who lived about a thousand years later— where Moses listens to him expounding the "law according to Moses." Moses is at a loss as he realizes that Rabbi Akiva is explaining many principles and *halakhot* (laws) that he has never heard of, and he is comforted only when Rabbi Akiva

> When Moses ascended on high, he found the Holy One engaged in extending the letters of Torah with cresting tittles and squiggles. Asked Him Moses: "Master of the world! Who will check You?" Said He to him: "In times to come after many generations a certain man called Akiva ben Yosef will articulate out of each crest minute details of *halakhah*." Moses requested to be shown this sage. God told him: "Retrace your steps!" And Moses found himself sitting in the last row. When he could not grasp what they were discussing, he was close to fainting. At a certain point of the discussion the disciples challenged Rabbi Akiva: "Whence this *halakhah*?" He replied: "It derives from the *halakhah* that Moses received from Sinai." Thus Moses' mind was put at ease.
>
> TB, *Menachot* 29b

assures one of his students: "This is the halakhah that Moses received from Sinai" *(halakhah le'moshe mi'sinai).*

The story teaches us something about the primacy of creative interpretation and its innovative function in the establishment of meaning, which is to say that the significance of "the book" *(byblos)* originates in what comes "after it" rather than in what precedes it. In other words, neither for Moses nor for Rabbi Akiva is "the book" (the Torah) in fact a book; rather, it consists of an oral teaching kept alive throughout the generations. The ramifications, meaning, and authority of this teaching grow within the interaction between students and their teachers. A traditional Islamic saying—much cited by medieval Jewish philosophers—remains true to this way of learning: We learn from the mouths of our teachers, not from books (*mipi soferim ve'lo mipi sefarim*). Thus, the significance of "the book"—and, I would say now, of any book—originates in its successive readings and commentaries. As Rosenzweig claims

> Written texts are but codes through which greater meanings are conveyed . . . , doorways through which pass communication between speaker and listener. . . . Truly to understand a text is to live in the middle of it, hearing with our own ears the voice of revelation and education. Paradise is not so much a geographical location as it is a sensory location of hermeneutics.
> Philip L. Culbertson,
> *A Word Fitly Spoken*   [4]

in one of his letters to Rudolf Ehrenberg, the significance of any great work originates with its translation.[8] Therefore, any biblical passage is grounded in its translations and commentaries, in Onkelos, the commentaries of Rashi, the *Mikra'ot Gedolot*, and the countless commentaries following them in successive acts of interpretation. Within this continuum of infinite creations of meaning— meaning "that always continues to be produced"[9]—any interpretation leaves a question mark inviting further readings. Hermann Cohen's entire "philosophy of origin" might be seen as revolving around the creative function of that "question mark"—a "nought of knowledge" in which new meaning originates.

The Sages refer to the multiplicity of meaning resulting from this open form of discourse in the much-cited dictum "there are seventy faces to the Torah" *(shiv'im panim la'torah)*. The biblical text itself thereby turns out to be the least authoritative of all—in fact, in a way, it does not really exist, since its presence originates with commentary. In the same vein, the Talmudic scholar would claim that when studying the "texts" of the oral tradition, primarily Mishnah and Gemara, it is the process of studying itself—in traditional terms,

> When the gentiles—who use all sorts of Bible translations each claiming to represent the literal meaning of the original text—ask you to explain to them some of the Midrashic interpretations of our Sages, they will refute you, saying: "You are twisting what we know to be written in scripture." They will refute you in this manner because they have erased the "seventy faces of the Torah" in which we discover multiple meanings.
> Shelomo ibn Parchon,
> *Machberet ha'Arukh*   [5]

"studying the Torah for its own sake" *(torah lishmah)*—that constitutes the aim of Talmudic studies and not the practical halakhic decision—the *psak*—by reference to which the ambiguity and multiplexity of the discussion are temporarily resolved.

Two Theses of the Religion of Reason

In Cohen's introduction to his *Religion of Reason,* we find two theses working toward a definition of the Jewish religion and its uniqueness: (a) that "the creativity of the concept" constitutes the originality and essence of Judaism; and (b) that "Jewish sources" are a living organism produced by oral discourse.

The Creativity of the Concept

Cohen maintains that the very acts of interpretation and of criticism— both of which are acts of "calling into question"—create the infinity of content that characterizes Jewish oral tradition, whereas any religious truth-claim produced by history, dogma, or emotional conviction turns out to be a mere derivative, a limited reading of the biblical tradition, presented in the garb of absolute religious truth. Such a dogmatic reading—if endowed with political, social, or religious authority—harbors the dangers of violence and totalitarianism, since the authority of its defenders tends to be as unbending as the "absoluteness" of their truth-claims. Cohen condemns such dogmatic limitation of the biblical text, calling it "idol worship" *(avodah zara),* in accordance with the classical Jewish definitions of this phrase. "Idol worship" in this context is characterized by a loss of "originality," resulting in a closure of the text, betraying the Jewish tradition of innovative interpretation and of creative textual reasoning. The term *originality,* or *origin,* is defined in Cohen's logic as the infinite creativity of human resourcefulness and critical reasoning. Consequently, Cohen's "philosophy of origin" has nothing to do with the concepts of "cause" in the Aristotelian sense or of "causality" in Newtonian physics, both of which denote a movement "from the past toward the future." In contrast, the concept of "origin" refers to the "limit of knowledge" by what has not yet been explored (represented by the "question mark"— the "nought of knowledge"). The

The logical significance of "the question" lies in its being the fulcrum of origin. . . . Critical judgment must not shy away from an adventurous detour. . . . "Nothing-

"nought of knowledge" constitutes the "origin" of what is known—or better still, of what will be known. The primacy of this principle—to

> ness" produces this adventure in thinking.
> Hermann Cohen,
> *Logik der reinen Erkenntnis* [6]

which Cohen refers as "the new thinking"[10] and which acquires a modified meaning in Rosenzweig's *Sprachdenken*—implies a way of interpreting religious traditions in which the past is predicated upon the future. To this way of thinking, nothing is "given" but the originality of the interpretation that links the facts into a coherent, objective structure. Thus we may say that "radical subjectivity" (although this is an entirely un-Cohenian phrase)—anchored in the originality of thinking—expresses itself in the construction of objectivity. According to Cohen, this process is the source

> In any case, in the realm of art the subjective and the objective are intertwined to the point of indistinction, ... the subjective settles into the objective and is reactivated into spontaneity by the touch of a genius.
> Thomas Mann,
> *Doktor Faustus* [7]

of all the sciences, including the natural sciences: Their "objectivity" is predicated upon a hermeneutical agenda prior to the "facts." There is a midrash, an ancient Jewish narrative, that appears to suggest that the "uncovering" of truth—the midrash uses the Greek word *aletheia*—originates in an act of subjectivity, namely that of creative interpretation.

> And what did God do? He threw the truth down to earth. ... Said his ministering angels to Him: "Lord of Worlds, what are you doing to your *aletheia*?" Whereupon God replied: "Let the truth grow out of earthliness, as it is written: 'truth grows out of the soil'" (Ps. 85:13).
> *Bereshit Rabba* [8]

According to Cohen's introduction to his *Religion of Reason*, the logical primacy of innovative interpretation—that is, the "originality of the concept"—is predicated upon two fundamental principles of the Jewish faith, namely "monotheism" and "messianism." Judaism, according to Cohen, originates with a peculiar reading of Jewish literature that hinges on the idea of the unique God. In other words, the very specificity of the Jewish tradition—and therewith the specificity of Talmudic discourse—is predicated upon an idea of transcendence. This idea of transcendence, however, is of a radically critical nature. God in His nonidentity with anything that exists—"to whom can you liken Me, and to whom can I be compared?" (Isa. 40:25)—burdens us with the cognitive task of critical thinking, a thinking that expresses itself in a continuous process of protest against the strictures of dogma. It is concerning the false pretenses of religious authority that it is written: "Tear down their altars, smash their pillars, . . . and cut down the images of their gods" (Deut. 12:3).

The ideal limit of this process of liberation is the "messianic age." Messianism constitutes the social and political implementation of Cohen's "principle of anticipation," directed toward the infinite task of creating a just society. The pursuit of justice and humanity, in the midst of the miserable privations that characterize our social world, draws its power of defiance precisely from the trust in the unalterable "ought" of these ideals. Cohen calls this trust in the authority of the "ought of the good" the "futurity of the ideal." The resistance to violence and "idolatrous" power structures originates in the vision of the ideal, of what is not yet but ought to be. In other words, the act of innovative, critical interpretation is predicated upon the ethical and hermeneutical priority of the "future" over the "past." Our critical judgment begins when we relate things as they are to the way they ought to be.

> Anticipation is the fundamental activity of time. . . . The past is predicated upon the future that is anticipated. It is not the past that is prior to thinking but rather the future.
> Hermann Cohen,
> *Logik der reinen Erkenntnis*   [9]

> It is incredible that messianism defies all political pragmatism and denigrates reality, treating it with contempt, annihilating it without mercy, replacing this sensible presence with a new kind of supersensibility, . . . that is, with futurity. . . . The great contribution of messianism is its creation of the future, representing, in effect, the true political reality. And this creation can only be the result of monotheism itself.
> Hermann Cohen,
> *Religion of Reason*   [10]

Cohen's "Jewish Sources": The Priority of Oral Discourse

In his introduction to the *Religion of Reason,* Cohen treats the entire literature of rabbinic tradition—which he calls "Jewish national literature"—as a living organism created by the specificity of the Jewish "national spirit." This "national spirit," Cohen emphasizes, is no "local spirit": "It is not localized in Zion; . . . but rather, wherever the Talmud is alive, the Torah is alive."[11] Oral tradition, accordingly, constitutes the living well of Jewish tradition, as its spontaneous method of interpretation attests to the inexhaustibility of meaning provided by the written texts. In other words, Jewish tradition consists of "open texts," always suggestive of more than a single interpretation, which means that no reading can claim to present a "full understanding" dictated by the story.[12] Cohen refers to this "infinity of text," or "inexhaustibility of meaning" produced by oral tradition, as "revelation." "Books tend to get sealed," Cohen says, "whereas mouths and lips go on speaking."[13]

> The "oral teaching" is not a finished product, but rather an open one, one that always continues to be produced. The book gets sealed; the mouth continues to speak; for the sake of the national spirit it must not become silent.
>
> Hermann Cohen, *Religion of Reason* [11]

Cohen advances the originality of oral tradition in terms of a classical Talmudic principle: *halakhah le'moshe mi'sinai*—which is to say that "the halakhah is part of the original revelation to Moses from Sinai." Far from attributing any "historicity" to the origins of halakhah, he reads this Talmudic term philosophically as the "creativity of reason" and hermeneutically as the unending process of innovative interpretation. In ac-

> And Rabbi Yehoshua ben Levi says: "Even what the adept student in the future shall expound in front of his teacher is part of the Torah that has been taught to Moses on Sinai."
>
> *Talmud Yerushalmi* [Jerusalem Talmud], *Peah* 2:6

cordance with a long-standing Jewish tradition of "negative theology," Cohen denies that any "positive knowledge" of the full content of divine revelation is humanly possible: Any such "positive theology" by definition must consist of fundamentalist theologoumena that lend themselves easily to the imposition of power over others and to intolerance of any "voice that differs." The "inner core" of the Jewish religion must therefore remain "pure"—that is, "free" of any such idolatrous positivity. It must remain free of idolatrous positivity, just as Israel's God must not align Himself with the positivity of any "local god" incarnated in the flesh, taking sides and fighting wars, and demanding sacrifice and the death of sinners.

According to Cohen, the specificity of the Jewish religion lies in its idea of the one and unique God who transcends manifestation, just as the specificity of Jewish tradition consists in its method of practicing oral tradition, which transcends any positivity of content. Both features correlate with each other, and together they constitute the "inner, inalienable core" of the Jewish religion. Based upon these

> God addressed Himself to the peoples of the world, saying: "How can you claim to be my children? Know that I consider as such only the keepers of my 'mysterium.'" Thereupon they inquired: "So what is your 'mysterium'?" He replied: "It is the *Mishnah*, which is all about the art of interpretation."
>
> *Pesiqta Rabbati* [12]

"pillars of faith," Judaism works continuously to demythify its own tribal origins. The local god of the "ancient Hebrews"—if there ever was one—can be of no more interest to the Jewish people than any other pagan god, whereas the "Lord of the Universe," demanding *chesed tsedakah u'mishpat*—"lovingkindness, justice, and truthfulness"[14]—has social and political relevance for all mankind.

Subsequently, Cohen defines Judaism as a religion characterized by the ideality of the law; in other words, Jewish law is committed to advancing the ideal of messianism, a commitment that translates into the pursuit of universal justice and

> The Halakhah is . . . the law of society as it should be—and . . . whoever fulfills it in fact establishes, as it were, a small forward bastion of the ultimate future in the present. . . . Jewish lawfulness is Messianic lawfulness, [and] . . . the Halakhah is religiously a permanent revolution.
> Steven S. Schwarzschild,
> *The Pursuit of the Ideal*   [13]

peace among the nations. Only under such premises does a renewed Talmudic mode of discourse ensure that Jewish law itself will not become an idolatrous tool of political intolerance and injustice.

Cohen's "New Thinking" and Rosenzweig's Sprachdenken

Franz Rosenzweig adopted Cohen's "new thinking," as indicated by the title of his much-cited essay of 1925 ("The New Thinking"). In fact, the revolutionary, "Jewish" mode of thinking so characteristic of Rosenzweig's *Star of Redemption,* which Levinas acknowledges as a central influence on his own philosophy, is indebted to Cohen's "philosophy of origin," into which Rosenzweig introduced ingenious modifications.

In his interpretation of Cohen's "new thinking," Rosenzweig inaugurated a philosophical revolution that, in fact, transcends the "literal meaning"—the *peshat*—of Cohen's logic, while keeping its method alive. Rosenzweig simply radicalizes Cohen's own claim concerning the creative power of "alterity"—in other words, of "otherness," or "that which differs." For Cohen, "alterity" is identical with the "limit of thought"; it is a "nought of knowledge" that assumes creativity in that it triggers a process in which "pure thinking" produces meaning that is ever new. Rosenzweig, however, reads "alterity" or "the nought of knowledge" as the end of thought—that is, the end of "my" thoughts.

Drawing upon Cohen's idea that "the I originates with the You,"[15] Rosenzweig claims that the other person, the concreteness of the other's face and voice, interrupts the vector of my thinking in a way that I never could have anticipated. In response to the other's face[16] and voice, even my own thinking becomes unpredictable—as it originates with an oral address initiated by another. Rosenzweig emphasizes the "complete passivity" of thought that is grounded in the other's act of speech. Just as for Cohen in his "method of origin," for Rosenzweig, too, it is the "question" that assumes the prime function of creative origin. But this time it is not the question posed in science, probing into what has not yet been explored. It is rather the

> In the new thinking, the method of speech replaces the method of thinking. . . . Thinking is timeless and wants to be timeless. . . . Speech is bound to time and nourished by time. . . . It does not know in advance just where it will end. It takes its cues from others. I do not know what the other person will say to me, because I do not even know what I myself am going to say. . . . "Speaking" means speaking to someone and thinking for someone. And this someone is always a quite definite someone, and he has not merely ears like "all the world," but also a mouth.
>
> Franz Rosenzweig,
> *The New Thinking* [14]

concrete question posed to me by another person that initiates the process of my "becoming a new self," a process of responsibility grounded in the other person's demanding my response.

In summary: Rosenzweig develops a genuinely philosophical theory of intersubjectivity based upon Cohen's hermeneutical claim concerning the primacy of oral tradition—"books are sealed, but the mouth keeps on speaking"—and expanding upon Cohen's ethical claim that the self originates in a "messianic" process of responsibility toward others.[17]

From Cohen to Post-Talmudic Hermeneutics

Concerning any future "philosophy of post-Talmudic hermeneutics," it is desirable that Talmudists should lead the discussion—which is why, at this stage of the project, I would like to leave the field to those of my colleagues who are more at home in the Talmud and the Midrash.

> Blessed is one whose mouth gives new interpretation and meaning to the words of the Torah within the academies grown numerous in Israel. Such a person is as if inspired by a heavenly voice saying: "My child, my great academy is yours," as it is said: God commends the innovations taught in the gates of learning (Judg. 5:8).
>
> *Seder Eliyahu Rabba* 11 [15]

As my own life and studies are primarily rooted in the German Jewish philosophical tradition, you may permit me, however, to

plead for keeping the post-Talmudic discussion connected to philosophical discourse, lest our discussion be adulterated by unconscious
expressions of dogmatism and of emotional bias. Philosophy, after
all, remains the guardian of critical reasoning. Let us remember that
Judaism leaves its own inner core open, protecting it from the kind
of "positivity" that assumes idolatrous powers. In Cohenian terms,
the openness of that "inner core" of Israel is ideally an openness toward self-criticism, providing room for the "voice that differs" and
instilling into our souls an absolute concern with human suffering.
And let us remain aware that when talking about a "pluralistic
hermeneutics" or a "polyphony of voices" we are indebted to Rosenzweig's theoretical preoccupation with Cohen's "method of origin,"
which Rosenzweig advances toward a theory of intersubjectivity in
which an "infinity of origins"—that is, an infinite number of particular faces—indicate the limits of the self (myself). Based upon the cultural project of the "new thinking," we may thus succeed in establishing a hermeneutical discussion of post-Talmudic methods that
affirms a multiplicity of personal ways to verify the truth without
falling into the trap of subjective relativism.

The voice of the late Emmanuel Levinas continues and advances
this project.[18] In Levinas, the project of the "new thinking" is concerned with translating the Talmudic method into the idioms of
Western culture by means of a hermeneutical agenda that is not only
indebted to the Western philosophical tradition but is also committed to addressing the impasses of that tradition. In Cohenian terms,
we could say that post-Talmudic studies cannot just be committed to
the "study of the Talmud for the Talmud's sake" but rather should
be dedicated to the "study of the Talmud for humanity's sake." To
invoke a typically Cohenian expression, "Wherever you find Israel's
preoccupation with the Torah mentioned in tradition, you should actually read 'Israel's preoccupation with humanity.'"

Note that our agenda of post-Talmudic studies is neither apologetic nor assimilationist in nature: It insists upon the specificity of
Jewish and Talmudic culture and upon the responsibility of Jews to
engage in that culture. Post-Talmudic discourse, however, is committed also to an even greater task: namely, that of translating methods and cultural habits that grow out of "Jewish particularity" into
the context of contemporary human culture, whose sufferings weigh
heavily upon our philosophizing.

Notes

1. In the course of this essay, I adopt a "textual practice" that was fully developed and brought to perfection by the printers of the Babylonian Talmud, who placed "windows" of text inside columns of commentary, demonstrating the atemporal concurrence of text and commentary, which is a fundamental principle of the Jewish oral tradition. Among Jewish scholars who have adopted this Talmudic layout is Robert Gibbs, in *Correlations in Rosenzweig and Levinas,* where Gibbs's commentary artfully surrounds singular "windows" of a text by Gabriel Marcel (see *Correlations in Rosenzweig and Levinas* [Princeton: Princeton University Press, 1992], chapter 9). The windows in this essay are meant as an invitation to the reader to personally become engaged in the discussion: They represent accompanying voices, often in the form of a traditional Jewish source, or express spontaneous literary associations. Visually, the reader thus faces the challenge of meeting with two differing texts, placed side by side, with no attempt being made to "close the gap" between them. Closing the gap between two differing voices, however, is precisely the task of new commentary—which must now be supplied by the reader.

2. Hermann Cohen, *Logik der reinen Erkenntnis*, ed. Helmut Holzhey, *Hermann Cohen Werke*, vol. 6/1 (Hildesheim: G. Olms, 1997).

3. Hermann Cohen, *Ethik des reinen Willens*, ed. Helmut Holzhey, intr. Steven S. Schwarzschild, *Hermann Cohen Werke,* vol. 7/2 (Hildesheim: G. Olms, 1981).

4. Cohen calls his philosophical method a "method of origin" (see *Logik der reinen Erkenntnis*, pp. 31–38 and 79–93; Helmut Holzhey, *Cohen und Natorp,* vol. 1, *Ursprung und Einheit* (Basel: Schwabe, 1986) pp. 175–201.

5. Franz Rosenzweig, *Der Stern der Erlösung*, intr. Reinhold Mayer (Frankfurt: Suhrkamp, 1990); *The Star of Redemption*, tr. William Hallo (New York: Holt, Rinehart and Winston, 1970).

6. Emmanuel Levinas, *Totality and Infinity: An Essay on Exteriority*, tr. Alphonso Lingis (The Hague: M. Nijhoff, 1969).

7. See the works of the incisive Italian interpreter of Hermann Cohen, Pierfrancesco Fiorato, and those of the master of the field, Helmut Holzhey, of Zürich.

8. Letter cited in Nahum N. Glatzer, ed., *Franz Rosenzweig: His Life and Thought* (New York: Schocken, 1961), pp. 62–63.

9. Hermann Cohen, *Religion of Reason out of the Sources of Judaism*, tr. Simon Kaplan, intr. Leo Strauss (New York: Ungar, 1972), p. 28.

10. Hermann Cohen, *Logik der reinen Erkenntnis*, p. 34.

11. Hermann Cohen, *Religion of Reason*, p. 28. I have slightly modified the translation.

12. See Avi Sagi, "Both Are the Words of the Living God: A Typological Analysis of Halakhic Pluralism," in *Hebrew Union College Annual* LXV, 1994, pp. 105–136.

13. Hermann Cohen, *Religion of Reason.*

14. Moses Maimonides, *The Guide of the Perplexed*, tr. Shlomo Pines, intr. Leo Strauss (Chicago: University of Chicago Press, 1963), p. 638.

15. Hermann Cohen, *Religion of Reason*, pp. 14–15.

16. Franz Rosenzweig, *Der Stern der Erlösung*, pp. 49, 464–471. Rosenzweig's *Gesicht* in the first reference was infelicitously translated by William Hallo as "vision" (*The Star of Redemption*, p. 45), obscuring the concept of "face" that Rosenzweig introduces there, in the sense of an "original singularity beyond the limits of thought."

17. Hermann Cohen, *Ethik des reinen Willens*, pp. 258–262 et passim.

18. Levinas's roots in the teachings of Rosenzweig—and via Rosenzweig in the teachings of Cohen—may account for much of Levinas's critique of Husserl and Heidegger, who are deeply associated with his philosophy.

References

[1] Emmanuel Levinas, *Nine Talmudic Readings*, tr. and intr. Annette Aronowicz (Bloomington: Indiana University Press, 1990), p. 91.

[2] Thomas Mann, *Dr. Faustus: Das Leben des deutschen Tonsetzers Adrian Leverkühn erzählt von einem Freunde* (Frankfurt am Main: Fischer, 1971), pp. 79, 375.

[3] Franz Rosenzweig, "Das neue Denken," in *Kleinere Schriften* (Berlin: Schocken, 1937), p. 376. (The translation is my own.)

[4] Philip L. Culbertson, *A Word Fitly Spoken: Context, Transmission, and Adoption of the Parables of Jesus* (Albany: State University of New York Press, 1995), pp. 49–50.

[5] Shelomo ibn Parchon, *Machberet ha'Arukh*, p. 11b, at the very end of *Chelek ha-Diqduq*. I am quoting the uncensored version, based upon an early manuscript at the Hebrew University, Jerusalem, the text of which I saw in the annotated copy of *Machbereth ha'Arukh* (ed. Salomon G. Stern [Pressburg: A. E. von Schmidt, 1844; repr. 1930]) belonging to my teacher, Z. Gotthold.

[6] Hermann Cohen, *Logik der reinen Erkenntnis*, ed. Helmut Holzhey, *Hermann Cohen Werke*, vol. 6/1 (Hildesheim: G. Olms, 1997), pp. 83–84.

[7] Thomas Mann, *Dr. Faustus*, p. 191.

[8] *Midrash Bereshit Rabba*, eds. Jehuda Theodor and Chanokh Albeck (Jerusalem: Jerusalem, 1996), p. 60.

[9] Hermann Cohen, *Logik der reinen Erkenntnis*, p. 154.

[10] Hermann Cohen, *Die Religion der Vernunft aus den Quellen des Judentums* (Leipzig: G. Fock, 1919), pp. 338–339. (The translation is my own.)

[11] Hermann Cohen, *Die Religion der Vernunft aus den Quellen des Judentums* (Leipzig: G. Fock, 1919), pp. 32–33. (The translation is my own.)

[12] *Midrash Pesiqta Rabbati*, ed. Meir Friedman (Ish Shalom) (Vienna: Selbstverlag, 1880), p. 14b.

[13] Steven S. Schwarzschild, *The Pursuit of the Ideal: Jewish Writings of Steven Schwarzschild*, ed. Menachem Kellner (Albany: State University of New York Press, 1990), pp. 75–76.

[14] Franz Rosenzweig, "Das neue Denken," tr. Nahum N. Glatzer, in *Franz Rosenzweig: His Life and Thought* (New York: Schocken, 1961), pp. 199–200.

[15] *Seder Eliyahu Rabba ve-Seder Eliyahu Zutta*, ed. Meir Friedman (Ish Shalom) (Jerusalem: Bamberger & Wahrman, 1960), p. 55.

8

Trends in Postmodern Jewish Philosophy: Contexts of a Conversation

Edith Wyschogrod

The extraordinary dialogue among Bob Gibbs, Steve Kepnes, Peter Ochs, and (briefly) Yudit Greenberg fastens upon significant aspects of postmodern thought in the interest of developing a new Jewish theology. Several motifs wind through their reflections: the transformation of ethics from an emphasis upon theory to a concern with alterity or the other human being; the depiction of the sedimentation and desedimentation of traditional texts as well as the relation between world and text; a turning away from analyzing the meaning of being to tracking the signs of interruption, the breaks, rifts, or fissures in language and being that open a discursive space for revelation; and, most striking, a reassessment of the relation of the Shoah to Jewish thought and practice. In its articulation of the Jewish themes of creation, revelation, and redemption—albeit in postmodern fashion—the present conversation appears to be conducted under the sign (Lyotard's phrase for a semiological web that articulates a theme) of Franz Rosenzweig. I shall consider first the modernist background of this conversation and then the postmodern articulations of the issues I have enumerated.

Modernity and Jewish Thought

The difficulty of drawing a boundary between modernism and postmodernism infiltrates the comments of the conversation partners at every level.[1] Jean-François Lyotard claims that the totalizing master narratives of modernism suppress the contingencies of aberrant experience such that social and linguistic context are stretched to fit such experience by interpreting it pejoratively as errant.[2] The participants agree that what sets postmodernism apart from modernism is the non-totalizing and nondichotomizing aspect of this thought. Yet beyond such consensus, the postmodern critique of totalization is open to multiple interpretations. Thus, for example, Peter believes it is not the matter of unity itself that is in question for postmodernity, but rather that of closure or finality, whereas Steve thinks that the issue is a passing away of the autonomous self of modernity as a unified center.

Of course, neither the texts nor the ethos of modernity have disappeared. Jürgen Habermas identifies modernism with the *Aufklärung's* vision of cognitive objectivity, and of universality in the applicability of moral rules and the principle of democratization in social and political affairs. In a statement that could almost have been drafted as a manifesto for liberal modernist Judaism, Habermas writes:

> The project of modernity, formulated in the 18th century by the philosophers of the Enlightenment, consisted in their efforts to develop objective science, universal morality and law, and autonomous art according to their inner logic. . . . The Enlightenment philosophers wanted to utilize [the] accumulation of specialized culture for the enrichment of everyday life—that is to say, for the rational organization of everyday social life.[3]

Liberal modern Jewish theology has drawn upon what is perhaps the grandest of Enlightenment modernity's metanarratives, that of Kantian and post-Kantian philosophy. Moses Mendelssohn, Kant's contemporary, offered a Jewish theological version of this narrative, one continuous also with an older tradition of natural theology, when he argued that Judaism's belief in God's existence and just governance of the world are in conformity with the requirements of reason, and thus are available to all rational beings. Revelation in Judaism, he contends, pertains to a code of laws applicable to Jews, but religion lies outside the sphere of what is revealed and it is accessible to reason. Religion thus construed is common to Jew and non-Jew alike.[4]

The intent of Kantian philosophy is continued in Hermann Cohen's exposition of ethical monotheism. Humankind is engaged in an infinite task of self-betterment—a task that is, on the one hand, a demand of reason, but on the other, unlikely to succeed, because the world by its very nature frustrates such rational directives. Thus, Cohen argues, if the requirements of reason are to be realized and ethical striving allowed to continue, there must be some guarantee of the ongoing character of humankind and world, a guarantee supplied by the idea of God.[5] Mendelssohn's and Cohen's Judaism carry on the Enlightenment project of individual ethical perfectionism and general social progress.

In the participants' consideration of the Enlightenment, Steve maintains that its effect upon Judaism was a subordination of the particular to the universal, whereas postmodernism's valuing of difference encourages a return to Judaism. Peter argues that Enlightenment philosophy is critique, and that by contrast, postmodernism is healing, recuperative, and compassionate. Bob points out that the Enlightenment project does not fail to take note of suffering but that its compassion excludes the other and remains self-referential. Bob is right in the main, yet the latitude of Kant's sympathy is worth noting. Kant writes:

> The injustice that [the civilized and commercial states] show to lands and people that they visit (which is equivalent to conquering them) is carried by them to terrifying lengths. America, the lands inhabited by the Negro, the Spice Islands, the Cape etc. at the time of their discovery were considered by these civilized intruders as lands without owners, for they counted the inhabitants as nothing. Under the pretense of establishing economic undertakings, they brought in foreign soldiers and used them to oppress the natives, excited widespread wars among the various states, spread famine, rebellion, perfidy and the whole litany of evils which afflict mankind.[6]

The verificationist model of truth in science and the claim that humankind as a whole is the reference point for moral action, both basic Enlightenment assumptions, are still endorsed by many Reform and Conservative Jews as well as by some Orthodox ones. But liberal Jewish theologian Eugene Borowitz has observed that these assumptions are incompatible with another value of modernity, that of personal autonomy and self-affirmation.[7] That value, I would argue, derives from another deep tendency of modernity, the turn to the subject—a tendency that persists even after the modernist ideals of truth and certainty are undermined on a number of fronts such as in the physical sciences, the philosophy of pragmatism, and for Jewish thought, early and mid-twentieth-century existential philosophies.

Although for existentialism the subject is a relational being constituted through her or his embeddedness in the world and through links with other persons, the way in which one exists as a subject remains the focus of existential thought. For the Jewish existentialism of Martin Buber, the "I" does not stand alone but either in a special connectedness with another person, a "Thou," or in relation to an object, an "It," so that a compound subject is formed. The "I" of "I-Thou" becomes what it is in living encounter with the other person or with the divine "Thou," whereas the "I" of "I-It" is the etiolated subject of cognition and utility. Thus, even if the subject waxes and wanes as the compound subject or primary word changes, it does not disappear.[8] What is more, the driving force of Buber's dialogic philosophy—to treat others as ends rather than as means—is ethical in the modernist Kantian sense, even if, for Buber, to do so does not entail obedience to the imperatives of Kantian practical reason.

Buber's "I-Thou" relation carries with it still another meaning that links it with the self of modernism—that of the "I's" self-renewal, the Romantic heritage of revitalization through ecstatic experience that leads not away from but toward a focus upon the self. When combined with the more heroic cast of Sartre's and Heidegger's existentialism (even if Jewish thinkers, wary of Heidegger's past, steer clear of any uncritical adoption of his analyses of human existence) and with Freudianism, the self remains central to modernist versions of Jewish thought. But existentialism's retention of the modern subject, however skillfully recast, does not withstand postmodern scrutiny.

If the quality of being a subject is the most persistent supposition of modernism (as Steve often and rightly notices), then the ethics of modernity must be an ethics of the subject. Right and wrong are attributed to the acts and motives of an autonomous self, a position that not only characterizes Kantian and neo-Kantian moral philosophy but also underlies various versions of utilitarianism—the Rawlsian notion of justice as well as the competing notions of many of his critics. If there can be a postmodern ethics—and it is difficult to imagine an ethics that circumvents the standard modes of argument and juridical reasoning—it must bypass the primacy of the subject.

This is, in fact, the course taken by Emmanuel Levinas, whose ethics stands at the cusp of modernism and postmodernism. For Levinas, ethics is Hebrew in its moral vision and Greek in the conceptual transposition of that vision. Ethics entails a leaching of self in its relation with the other such that the self places itself totally at the disposal of the other. (In his elaboration of Levinas's views, Bob highlights the radical character of the sacrifice of self in the interest of the other.) Exposure to the other is an openness to the preverbal appeal of the other's vulnerability and precedes the process of making decisions about specific moral questions. The relation with another who is always more than and exterior to oneself is not a prolegomenon to ethics but *is* already ethics.

Although Levinas's stress upon the ethical relation originates to some extent in Kantian moral philosophy by way of Hermann Cohen and as filtered by Franz Rosenzweig, it derives in important ways from a specific mode of interpreting classical Jewish sources—that of Lithuanian Jewry from the eighteenth century to the years just before World War II—in which the ethics of alterity and the emphasis upon compassion, charity, and generosity play a significant role.[9]

The World of the Text

Derridean postmodernisms are characterized by their turning to the text as the locus of signification and their rejection of the view that language is a transparent medium through which a world external to it can be made present. Although deconstructionists are not likely to state the idea in these terms, the text gives birth to the world rather than the converse. This privileging of the text is not an affirmation that there is nothing outside the text, a point stressed by Derrida, but rather a focus upon text as the site (or non-site) of meaning and as opening out into infinite interpretive possibilities. This notion is foreign to the traditions of Western philosophy but not to rabbinic thought with its underlying assumption that God consults the Torah to create the world (thus affirming that before the beginning there was the text). What is more, the written Torah is looked upon as an extreme condensation whose explication is unfolded in the Talmud and later rabbinic writings in an ongoing hermeneutical process, although not a process without rules. The blurring of the boundary between *what* is to be interpreted and its interpretation results in a vastly expanded textual field. Susan Handelman, one of the first to point out the affinities of postmodern and rabbinic interpretation, suggests in an earlier work, "This fluidity is a central tenet of much contemporary literary theory." Some postmodern literary interpreters, she contends, write commentaries that are secular versions of midrashim.[10]

Modernism's faith in the canons of reason has been replaced not only by postmodern skepticism, itself a tactic of traditional philosophy, but by the development of interpretive strategies that treat philosophy and the artifacts of culture in a new, often epistemically deconstructive fashion. It is by now a truism that there are multiple and often conflicting strands of postmodernism. Yet most postmodernists would agree that the classical issues of philosophy, especially as expounded by the German Enlightenment thinkers and their successors, are stories—metanarratives about being, time, and history—and not themselves the truth about these matters. This is not to say that postmodernists claim that modern philosophy is a tale told by an idiot, signifying nothing, but that modern philosophy promises what it cannot deliver, a narrative that turns to the subject of cognition as the source of truth.

These issues are not merely appropriated by postmodern Jewish thought in an effort to align itself with contemporary trends. Contrary to the argument that the spirit of postmodernism is an outcome of French dandyism's playfulness and affectations[11]—as manifest in the poetics of Baudelaire, Mallarmé, Artaud, Jarry, and others—postmodern thinking is, in fact, in no small measure the result of turning both to recent Jewish experience and to traditional Jewish modes of interpretation. Although they share little else, both recent French aesthetics and rabbinic hermeneutics lie outside literary critical orthodoxies and proceed otherwise than by way of the canons of standard philosophical discourse, appealing to association and a variety of rhetorical tropes as critical tools. What is more, both are in the position of outsiders. Although the aesthetics of nineteenth- and early twentieth-century French literature has its place in configuring postmodern thought, postmodernism is, in important respects, a creation of Jewish history and hermeneutics rather than a cluster of adopted strategies.

Like rabbinic exegesis, the present dialogue is free-form, ricocheting from one theme to another, looping around fragments of argument that are often metonymically rather than syllogistically linked. Unlike the Platonic dialogues with their sophistic villains and Socratic heroes, this is a discussion among companions in a friendship that is being established by learning together, and one that allows for considerable latitude. Although all the conversational partners move toward a non-Derridean postmodernism, the differences among them are significant when they reflect upon the compatibility of Judaism, however interpreted, with any given version of postmodernism. For Steve, postmodern Judaism has a *Sitz im Leben,* and cannot be confined to the house of study, because life and learning are continuous; Yudit points to postmodernism as an activity, a process that attends to the quality of relationships, and a style of thinking that presumably has consequences for life; Peter insists that postmodernism "corrects" modernism's inattentiveness to human suffering.

All of these assertions are less a concession to a postmodern, Rorty-like amalgam of American pragmatism (with its stress on experience) and French criticism than a response to Jewish history. The assertion "it happened," where "it" refers to the innumerable catastrophes and redemptive events of that history, is critical in the break with a pantextual deconstructive version of postmodernism in which factuality is obscured. Even Roland Barthes's radical claim that history is less a collection of facts than a relation of signifiers organized to establish positive meaning, cannot gainsay the referential dimension of that history. Yet it is the activity of textual interpretation, of immersion in Judaism's classical writings, that is redemptive. For most of these Jewish theologians, the study of Torah is an effort at synergy, at bringing God onto the page of the text in order to find redemption through a divine pedagogy that alters our discursive strategies and allows for new disclosures of the sacred. Thus, the text itself is redemptive. There is no epiphany other than the unveiling of textual meaning.

It may be useful to think of these texts as standing under the authority of what transcends them and thereby sacralizing the interpreter's hermeneutical acts. As Franz Rosenzweig wrote in a letter to Martin Buber: "The primary content of revelation is revelation itself." The falling into language of revelation, even the language of the first-person proclamation of transcendent presence, the "I am" of Exodus, is always already "the beginning of interpretation."[12]

If redemption is to be sought through the devotion to text, it is not as a dry exercise in *pilpul* (hairsplitting analysis) but rather as an affective relation to what is revealed in the text. Bob powerfully invokes grief and "the gate of tears"; Peter speaks of the pleasure of redemption through the pleasure of the text. It is unlikely that Peter has in mind the Dionysian, nonconceptual pleasure unpredetermined by conventions of reading to which Roland Barthes alludes when he uses this phrase but rather what Michel de Certeau intends when he describes St. Theresa's wandering through her interior castle and experiencing the joy of divine encounter. Yet what must remain paradoxical for postmoderns are the conflicting impulses of the experiential intensities of inwardness generated by interpretation, and the postmodern rejection of interiority.

I am moved but also troubled by the way in which the appeal to hermeneutical endeavor by the dialogue's participants is seen to exalt and redeem. Can a post-Holocaust return to the text be productive of joy (even if not unalloyed) any more than the vanished world of Hasidism that Buber tried to recreate? More disturbing is the absence of appeal to that internal Jewish Other who is excluded from learning for whatever reason, the *am h'aaretz* (man of the soil, or unlearned man) and the woman, both of whom historically and currently are barred from textual redemption and whose very names are signifiers of contempt. Are they not in the situation of the man in the tired but still pertinent joke who enters the synagogue on Rosh Hashanah without a ticket and is warned by the *shamus* (beadle) that he can come in, but God help him if he is caught praying. The reinforcement that a textually oriented postmodernism provides for the elite who study Torah should not be permitted to exclude the invisible other who has no regimen of phrases (in Lyotard's terms) with which to make her or his case. Should not the devotional registers of prayer and liturgy, open to all, enter into the economy of redemption, not only because they have traditionally (on any reading of tradition) done so, but on ethical grounds? After all, who can tell how the place cards are to be distributed for seats in the world to come (to use a rabbinic locution)?

Ethics and the Hunger for the Sacred

It is the hunger for the sacred in a post-Shoah, postmodern world that constitutes the affective subtext not only of Jewish learning but also of Jewish ethics. When ethics is interpreted as a theory about the good life or as the construction of norms of conduct, affective attachments are ruled out as irrelevant to the framing of principles, as the rationalist tradition of ethics from Plato to Kant attests. Received interpretations of Kant stress that even if we cannot know things as they are in themselves, we can at least be sure about the boundaries of our knowledge and we can be clear about what is right and wrong in the moral realm. Because liberal Jews as well as the giants of recent Jewish thought—Rosenzweig, Buber, and Levinas—write under the sign of Kant, for whom ethics must remain disinterested, the pain felt at the destitution of the other is obscured. For postmoderns, the tension between affect and disinterest is heightened, a tension that is captured in Bob's phrase, "to intensify ethics." French postmodernism's stress on desire—from Lacan to Deleuze, from Derrida to Kristeva and Irigaray—as well as the emphasis on affect in Jewish existentialism suggests a libidinal quest for an elusive object that runs directly counter to the Kantian description of practical reason.

Postmodern Jewish philosophy locates the concerns of ethics neither in the analysis of specific problems nor in the discovery of universal laws but in the radical shattering of "my" world through "my" relation to the other person. As a field of moral concern, the other lies beyond comprehension, cannot be incorporated into concepts or narratives, but imposes a moral response. To be sure, the Kantian impulse to retain disinterestedness militates against a relation to pure alterity; yet it cannot go unnoticed that for Levinas, the other comes crashing into one's world, opening the "gate of tears." What is more, Kant's formless and figureless imperatives are supplanted by the figure of the unfigurable, the face of the other, which despite Levinas's caveats about its aniconicity, attains ethical significance because the other is a vulnerable being of flesh and blood.

Without entering into the fine points of Lyotard's postmodern treatment of Kant's *Critique of Judgment,* postmodern Jewish thinkers might want to respond to Lyotard's admittedly dangerous text. The text suggests a way for postmodern Jewish ethics to avoid the difficulties imposed by the sediment of the universal and the juridical in practical reason. In the context of a discussion about the teleology of nature and related matters, Kant elaborates upon the difference between the beautiful and the sublime. The manner in which, for Kant, we arrive at aesthetic judgments is unhelpful, because Kant invokes the *sensus communis* in the realm of taste, which is analogous to the totality of rational beings in the realm of ethics. The beautiful is capable of symbolizing moral good and thus is ultimately under the aegis of practical reason. But the dangerous Kant entertains the possibility of disclosure through affect, through a feeling of the sublime, which captures without conceptualizing what is terrifying and what cannot be an object of thought. This situation arises when the imagination is confronted with a limitless Idea of

Reason and feels its limitation. The object of imagination "is appre-
hended as sublime with a joy which is only made possible by the me-
diation of pain," says Kant.[13] One of his examples, the feeling of
awe before a thunderstorm watched from the shelter of a cove, could
be a trope for the feeling of the interpreter before the sacredness of
the text. But can the sublime, in violation of Kant's own usage, be
applied to ethics? Transposed into a postmodern language of desire,
Bob's and Peter's comments on suffering would seem to imply that
the desire for the other is a complex of pain and pleasure, a feeling
of sublimity before a nonconceptualizable other.

Equally significant and challenging to postmodern Judaism is the
Nietzschean strand that dominates both French and American versions of postmodern thought. Peter comes closest to a Nietzschean
theology when he argues for a kind of self-overcoming or -tran-
scending—not on the part of human beings, as Nietzsche proposes,
but rather within the divine nature: The infinite must destroy itself,
give up its abstract infinity for the concrete power to heal. Thus,
God is both destroyer and redeemer. The cataclysms that Nietzsche
foresaw are now transposed to the sphere of God's own activity.

This is an extremely promising but not unproblematic line of
thought. Conceiving the infinite as destroyer and redeemer is a fa-
miliar theme in the history of religions. The pair are intrinsic to
many versions of Hinduism, envisaged as Shiva and Brahma, but in
that context, their unceasing alternation is a cosmological process.
Can the historical and messianic thrust of Judaism be rendered compatible with the noneschatological and cyclical character of such an
account?

It can also be argued that the identifying mark of Nietzschean
postmodernism is its sheer refusal to traffic in transcendence. Thus,
for example, Deleuze contends that for Nietzsche, the illusoriness of
transcendence consists either in rendering immanence immanent to
something other than itself or in locating transcendence within immanence.[14] To be sure, even if no one version of postmodernism is
definitive, Deleuze and other key figures who have opened the discursive space of postmodernism have written under the sign of
Nietzsche. In this context, Steve's admonition to resist first dis-
counting modernism and then returning to premodernity and calling
it postmodern is worth heeding. In sum, an explicit response is
needed to the radical immanentism of Nietzsche-inspired postmodernisms.

Holocaust and Negation

Modern Jewish thought founders not only because of its inner contradictions—the conflicting values of universality in ethics and the
egoity of the individual subject—but rather disintegrates for reasons
extrinsic to these philosophical tensions. It is the historical traumas
of the twentieth century that call the values of modernity into question: the eruption of two devastating world wars, the creation of So-
viet slave labor camps, the construction of Nazi concentration and
death camps, and numerous subsequent massacres, each replete with
its own species of horror. Although attributable largely to deep-
seated anti-Semitism, the building of the camps can be seen, at least
in part, as an outcome of modern social organization and new tech-
nologies rooted in modernist conceptual foundations. The Shoah is
generally acknowledged to open a new era, one in which the modes
of rationality invoked to explain the event fail to account for it while
at the same time they are seen as implicated in causing it.

In order to grasp the shift in sensibility that is under way in postmodern Jewish philosophy with regard to the Shoah, it is worth re-
hearsing the history of earlier responses. Emil Fackenheim, a key figure in bringing the Holocaust into theological focus, argues that it
defies ordinary historical explanation and precludes a return to any
traditional theodicy. The unprecedented extermination of an entire
people on racial grounds, Fackenheim maintains, shows that the for-
mative values of Western culture failed to prevent the emergence of
radical evil. He argues, further, that the fulfillment of Jewish commandments is a necessary response not to revelation but to the com-
manding voice of Auschwitz.[15] Not only does Richard Rubenstein
question the moral value of modernity's conceptual core, but he is
the first to suggest that the Holocaust is evidence for the power of
negation within the divine life itself.[16] His intent is not to reinstate
a discursive negation, a traditional negative theology that brings to
light the divine attributes, but to argue for a nihilatory power within
the divine nature. Along similar lines, Arthur Cohen treats the Holocaust as an apocalyptic event, the "tremendum" that erupts in the
order of being and time to create a caesura between what came before and after it.[17]

With the theological interpretations of the Shoah, a gap emerges
between the thought of modernity and postmodernity that goes far
beyond existentialism's critique of reason. This gap is the source not

only of an exclusively Jewish intrareligious meditation but also of an alteration in historical consciousness generally, a change that challenges the languages of description and analysis. The inadequacy of language becomes a focal point in the fiction of Elie Wiesel, Charlotte Delbos, and Edmond Jabès, and in the films of Claude Lanzmann, the goal of which is less to express the unsayable than to bring to the fore the problem of unsayability. When the unsayable is spoken in the straightforward language of journalism, its horror is flattened out; when it is mythologized, archetypal meanings are foisted upon it; when fictionalized, it is attributed to imaginary persons; when photographed, it becomes pornographic, and so on. Susan Shapiro, in an article about inexpressibility, has referred to Holocaust writing as "failing speech,"[18] a notion that is applicable to a number of postmodern writers—especially to those for whom the Shoah is implicitly and often explicitly a wedge into postmodernity.

The alteration in Jewish theology from the Shoah-centered reflection of the preceding generation to a postmodern theological conversation in which the Shoah appears to have passed from living memory into history is therefore especially striking. Although suffering is the acknowledged leitmotif of the new theology for Bob and Peter, there is no single historical event that any of the participants is willing to pinpoint as precipitating the centrality of suffering for postmodern Jewish theological thinking. What reasons can be adduced for this change in sensibility? Is it an application of deconstructive postmodernism's tenet that historical narratives preclude any focal point that creates an identity—in this case, the identity of a communal subject shaped by genocide? But in what is by now a "tradition" of postmodernism extending back to Adorno and passing through Lyotard and Blanchot, the *désastre* (to use Blanchot's term for the Shoah) is the nihilatory rift or fissure that cannot in any case become the center or focus of a narrative; so a worry about the Shoah as a fixed center fails to explain this shift. More likely, the interlocutors might feel that the Shoah becomes a way of avoiding the dailiness of life, the ordinary trivialities that are our lot. Or as some participants comment, the Shoah may blunt affective responses to the suffering of numerous others. In sum, the dialogue's participants for the most part limit the role of the Shoah to that of historical signpost to the failure of modernity—an end—but not to the new beginning that Jewish theology must undertake, a beginning that lies in a repossessing of Judaism's classical texts as the redemptive discourse of postmodernity.

But can Jewish theology "archive" the Shoah? Are there enough gigabytes of memory, so to speak, in Jewish and Western consciousness to hold this event? What is to become of the Shoah as memory passes into history? Is it to enter into the discursive space of theology, and if so, how? Perhaps the most suggestive response to date with regard to the question of theodicy and of how to go on is to be found in the words of the Master of the Universe in the text of *Menachot* 29b, cited by the participants in the conversation: "Silence. Thus it came to my mind."

NOTES

1. I use *modern philosophy* as a name for the tradition of Western thought from Descartes through Husserl, and *modernism* to designate the spirit that characterizes modern philosophy, principally its faith in reason. Although French postmodernists have thus far shown little interest in Anglo-American analytic philosophy, the development of logic as both a method and a theme of that philosophy would qualify much recent Anglo-American thought as a species of modernism, despite points made by some of its practitioners against modern philosophy that coincide with French postmodern criticisms. The terms *modern philosophy* and *modernism* will in some contexts be interchangeable. *Modernity* is used as a chronological concept and refers to the time frame in which the spirit of modernism develops.

2. Jean-François Lyotard, *The Postmodern Condition: A Report on Knowledge*, trans. F. Geoff Bennington and Brian Massumi (Minneapolis: University of Minnesota Press, 1984), pp. 31–37.

3. Jürgen Habermas, "Modernity versus Postmodernity," *New German Critique* 22, p. 9.

4. Moses Mendelssohn, *Jerusalem and Other Jewish Writings*, trans. Alfred Jospe (New York: Schocken Books, 1969), p. 61.

5. Hermann Cohen, *Religion of Reason out of the Sources of Judaism*, trans. Simon Kaplan (New York: Frederick Ungar, 1972), p. 70.

6. Immanuel Kant, *On History*, ed. Lewis White Beck (Indianapolis: Liberal Arts Press, 1963), pp. 103–104, paragraph 360.

7. Eugene Borowitz, *Renewing the Covenant* (Philadelphia: Jewish Publication Society, 1991), pp. 170–181.

8. Martin Buber, *I and Thou*, trans. Ronald Gregor Smith (New York: Scribner's, 1958), pp. 1–6.

9. For an account of the influence of Lithuanian Judaism, specifically that deriving from the followers of the *gaon* (genius) of Vilna, Rabbi Elijah ben Solomon, see Judith Friedlander, *Vilna on the Seine* (New Haven: Yale Uni-

versity Press, 1991). The work of a member of this school, Chaim of Volozhin, is of particular interest to Emmanuel Levinas.

10. Susan Handelman, *The Slayers of Moses* (New York: SUNY Press, 1982), p. 80. An important work establishing the connection between rabbinic exegesis and postmodern thought is Jose Faur's *Golden Doves with Silver Dots: Semiotics and Textuality in Rabbinic Tradition* (Bloomington: Indiana University Press, 1986).

11. This possible connection between French dandyism and postmodernism is suggested by Steven Best and Douglas Kellner in *Postmodern Theory: Critical Interrogations* (New York: Guilford Press, 1991), p. 16.

12. Letter dated June 5, 1955, in *On Jewish Learning*, ed. N. N. Glatzer (New York: Schocken, 1955), p. 118.

13. Cited in Jean-François Lyotard, "The Sign of History," trans. Geoff Bennington, in *Post-Structuralism and the Question of History*, eds. Derek Attridge, Geoff Bennington, and Robert Young (Cambridge: Cambridge University Press, 1987), p. 172.

14. Nietzsche's four great errors are identified as the illusion of transcendence, of universals, of eternity, and of discursiveness, the last bound up with Deleuze's elaboration of the difference between propositions and philosophical concepts, an issue that lies beyond the scope of these remarks. See Gilles Deleuze and Felix Guattari, *What Is Philosophy*, trans. Hugh Tomlinson and Graham Burchell (New York: Columbia Press, 1994), pp. 49–50. Walter Kaufmann summarizes Nietzsche's text describing the four idols *(Twilight of the Idols)* in Friedrich Nietzsche, *The Portable Nietzsche* (New York: Viking Press, 1969), vol. VI, pp. 492–501, as follows: (1) mistaking effects for causes, as when we say that people perish on account of their vices, instead of seeing their vices as consequences of the degeneracy of which they die; (2) assuming the false causality of spiritual causes such as will, consciousness, or ego; (3) introducing imaginary causes, such as in the invention of antecedents in dreams, to explain prior stimulus after the fact; (4) presupposing free will.

15. See Emil Fackenheim, *God's Presence in History* (New York: New York University Press, 1970), especially pp. 67–98.

16. Richard Rubenstein, *After Auschwitz* (Indianapolis: Bobbs-Merrill, 1966), pp. 46ff.

17. Arthur Cohen, *The Tremendum: A Theological Interpretation of the Holocaust* (New York: Crossroad, 1981), pp. 55–56.

18. Susan Shapiro, "Failing Speech: Post-Holocaust Writing and the Discourse of Postmodernism," *Semeia* 40, 1987.

Epilogue

We are indebted to our five respondents for their serious and generous critiques and commentaries. Since we received these responses, we have extended our dialogue to a variety of other public forums where we could elicit serious comment. Our thinking has become a product of dialogue not only with each other and the five respondents in this book but also with a larger number of conversational partners. In this epilogue, we reflect on the important effects these conversations have had on postmodern Jewish philosophy.

In the early 1990s, we established a postmodern Jewish philosophy electronic network via the Internet to allow us to keep in regular touch with each other from our different locations and to engage in a free-floating conversation with anyone who wanted to listen in and respond. We quickly found that at least some of what we were saying resonated with a significant number of people who "listened in" to our conversations by electronic mail, and we learned that these listeners were established scholars and graduate students, philosophers and text scholars, Jewish studies scholars and academics outside of our field, Jews as well as non-Jews. We later added an e-mail journal to give formal shape to our discussions. We have gathered regularly at meetings of the American Academy of Religion and of the Association for Jewish Studies, and we have arranged a number of other conferences for face-to-face Jewish philosophical discussions based on reading Jewish texts in a dialogic manner. In the process of defining ourselves as "postmodern Jewish philosophers," we learned that we needed conversation with various others: some of whom were not primarily trained in philosophy but in Jewish text scholarship, some of whom were not Jewish, and some of whom were not "postmodern" (indeed, these were people for whom the term "postmodern" was more of an obstacle than an invitation to converse with us).

Through our conversations it became clear that our differences from non-Jewish postmodern philosophy arose from our central concern with ethics and from our willingness and desire to think with and through the revealed texts of Judaism and rabbinic modes of interpreting them. The thinking that we do with and through and after the texts of revelation is not (as in modern Jewish philosophy) primarily to derive ethical and theological concepts that could be purified, modified, and "applied" to modern life but to learn again how to embody ethics and theology in all the things that we do as human beings living in communities. What we seek in postmodern Jewish philosophy is the intricate connection between right thinking and right living, a connection so deep and immediate that it cannot be articulated either as theory applied to practice or as the process "derive, purify, modify, apply." We find models for this connection in revelation as the rabbis understood it: as simultaneously text, commentary, and action.

At various stages along the way, as postmodern Jewish philosophy has further coalesced and developed through our relationships with new communities of colleagues, we have adopted new labels to identify what we do in these different, emerging contexts. We came to call the results of our conversations with colleagues primarily trained in Jewish text scholarship "textual reasoning." This is reasoning with and through the "revealed" Jewish texts of the written and oral Torah and their interpretations. *Textual reasoning* refers to the patterns of reasoning that emerge prototypically out of Talmudic/rabbinic practices of rereading or interpreting scripture. In rabbinic tradition, these are the patterns of "oral Torah" *(torah she b'al peh)* as opposed to the "written Torah" of scripture *(torah she b'khtav)*. For postmodern Jewish philosophers, these may be refigured as the patterns of textual reasoning that will replace principles of ethics, metaphysics, and epistemology that were previously derived from Western philosophic prototypes. Although textual reasoning is modeled on the practices of rabbinic text interpretation, it has analogues also in the interpretive traditions of the other scripture-based religions. A Society for Textual Reasoning was established to facilitate the electronic-mail journal, an e-mail "chat" network, and various face-to-face meetings of what for the previous seven years had been called the Postmodern Jewish Philosophy E-Mail Network. Although the Society was generated by scholars of Jewish texts and philosophy, it had begun to attract Christian theologians and philosophers as well.[1]

Fruitful conversations with an even wider range of philosophers and scholars trained in the Christian, Muslim, and Jewish scriptures led us to adopt the broader label of "scriptural reasoning" to encompass the parallel forms of reasoning with scripture that are being pursued across religious traditions. *Scriptural reasoning* refers to the patterns of reasoning that emerge out of philosophically disciplined readings of Holy Scriptures by Jews, Christians, and Muslims who seek alternatives both to the foundational or reductive discourses of secular academia and to the antimodern or extrarational religious fundamentalisms that sometimes replace them. Specific to its tradition of revealed text and communal interpretation, each pattern of scriptural reasoning also will be marked in some specific way, as "rabbinic scriptural reasoning," "Orthodox Christian scriptural reasoning," "Lutheran scriptural reasoning," and so on. A Society for Scriptural Reasoning was established in 1996 by Jewish, Christian, and Muslim thinkers who had begun to meet periodically for shared text study and interpretation.[2] These scripture-based forms of reasoning have augmented the continuing enterprise of relating and differentiating modern and postmodern philosophical methods and correlating them with Jewish thought. This enterprise continues as we interact with fellow Jewish and non-Jewish philosophers in such forums as the Academy for Jewish Philosophy, the American Philosophical Association, and the Society for Phenomenology and Existential Philosophy.

The process of definition in this book was not, therefore, simply an attempt to find the essence of "postmodern Jewish philosophy," as if knowing this essence would allow us to fix other things—Jewish philosophy, Judaism, the world. Postmodern Jewish philosophy is not a "something" but is a loose set of activities undertaken by various people in different groups in different ways. It is not an ideologically defined party but is rather an evolving orientation for thinking. That orientation is directed by a crisis of suffering in our times and a persistent concern to think and seek after what revealed Jewish texts and practices can teach.

The concern for an ethics that refuses a good conscience in the face of other people's suffering and an ethics that refuses complicity with others' suffering draws insight and inspiration from the Jewish tradition and from elsewhere. Thus, our postmodern Jewish philosophical activities are not separable from our various other conversations with groups of textual reasoners, scriptural reasoners, Jewish philosophers, and other sorts of postmodern philosophers. Like a tree, our thinking has grown various branches whose leaves overlap and nourish it. We have branched out in order to further the work that we are calling postmodern Jewish philosophy, and we have altered our labels in accordance with those with whom we are in conversation. This book, then, offers a snapshot of a growing tree—a tree that seeks to embrace the revealed Tree of Life, the Torah, at the same time that it seeks after the revealing truth for this generation in the face of excessive suffering and destruction.

We will close with a final word on the title of this book: *Reasoning After Revelation*. This phrase has a number of meanings for us. It means that we recognize that we come after the fixity of revealed texts of Jewish tradition and that a part of the enterprise of postmodern Jewish thinking involves thinking with these revealed texts to draw out their multiple meanings. But it also means that we come before revelation in the sense that its truths are not fixed in our minds, our hearts, and our actions, and that we must strive after the revelation, which remains (as Hermann Cohen reminds us) far out in front of us, as an ideal. However, between the fixity of a written Torah, which we come after, and the ideal Torah, which we seek after, are the positive moments of interpreting, understanding, and enacting Torah, which are also part of revelation. In appreciation of this fact, Buber, Levinas, and Rosenzweig talk about "continuous revelation." By continuous revelation they mean that revelation is a two-party term: not merely the gift of Torah but also the reception of Torah in the thought and action of those who, in their multiple and different ways, interpret it. This means that the reception of the revelation of God is part of the revelation. And the consolation (dare we say redemption!) of those of us who stand between the gift of the Torah of the past and the Torah of the messianic future is the fact that we can participate in the revelation of Torah today by receiving it. So we Jewish philosophers situate ourselves in postmodernity, yet simultaneously after, before, and thankfully, in the midst of revelation.

NOTES

1. The Society's founding directors are David Novak (University of Toronto) and Peter Ochs. The electronic Journal of Textual Reasoning is co-edited by Aryeh Cohen (University of Judaism), Charlotte Fonrobert (Syracuse University), Nancy Levene (Harvard University), Jacob Meskin (Princeton University), and Michael Zank (Boston University). Subscription and editorial information may be obtained on line from mzank@bu.edu.

The editors oversee an annual meeting of the Society in conjunction with the American Academy of Religion. Other associate editors (and associate directors of the Society) include Robert Gibbs, Steven Kepnes, Susan Handelman (University of Maryland), Laurie Zoloth-Dorfman (University of Judaism), Shaul Magid (Jewish Theological Seminary), Elliot Wolfson (New York University), Philip Culbertsen (St. John's, Auckland, New Zealand), Roger Badham (Drew University), and Ola Sigurdsen (University of Lund, Sweden).

2. The Society's founding directors are David Ford and Daniel Hardy (Cambridge University), Peter Ochs, Elliot Wolfson, and Robert Cathy (Monmouth College, Illinois), the last of whom chairs the Society's meetings, which are held in conjunction with the annual meeting of the American Academy of Religion. William Elkins (Drew University) currently directs the Society's Web site, which is based at Drew.

Glossary

Adorno, Theodor (1903–1969)   Leader of the Frankfurt School of critical theory, combining Marxist theory and cultural critique. Author of *Negative Dialectics* (1966).

aggadah   Homiletical interpretation in rabbinic Judaism, literally "telling"; contrasted with *halakhah,* or legal interpretation.

Akedah   The Binding of Isaac in the biblical account (Gen. 22), serving various homiletical meanings in rabbinic and later literature.

Akiva   Leading rabbi in the period of the earlier Sages *(Tannaim).* Expanded the role of Scriptural interpretation in Jewish religion and developed the organization of the Mishnah.

Amidah   The central prayer of Jewish liturgy, adopted by the rabbis to replace the daily sacrifices in the Temple. The *Amidah* is recited at least three times daily and has three parts: (1) praises of God's love, power, and holiness, as displayed to ancient Israel; (2) petitions for national and individual blessings; and (3) thanksgivings for prayer and for peace.

Baconian   Derived from the philosophical perspective of Francis Bacon (1561–1626), who called for a far-reaching empirical research program in the sciences.

Barthes, Roland (1915–1980)   French literary theorist and critic. Author of *Writing Ground Zero* (1953).

Benjamin, Walter (1892–1940)   Cultural critic whose writings on literature and on consumer culture were underappreciated during his lifetime but later became famous through publications organized by his friends, Adorno and Scholem. Benjamin's studies of vernacular culture suggest ways of "brushing history against the grain." His work has greatly influenced postmodern Jewish philosophy in its attentiveness to the political and cultural idiom of textual interpretation.

Bergson, Henri (1860–1941)   Assimilated French Jewish philosopher. Explored the structures of lived time.

143

Bernstein, Richard (b. 1932) Contemporary American philosopher of hermeneutics, political theory, and pragmatism.

Blanchot, Maurice (b. 1907) French writer and literary critic. Friend of Levinas. Author of *Writing the Disaster* (1980). Blanchot interprets how writing absents the author from the reader. His primary interest is in the tensions present in a text's immanence.

Borowitz, Eugene (b. 1924) Leading liberal Jewish theologian. Author of *Renewing the Covenant: A Theology for the Postmodern Jew* (1991). He has helped to stimulate postmodern Jewish theology through his call for liberal Jews to resituate their critical rationality within communities of rabbinic text interpretation.

Buber, Martin (1878–1965) German Jewish philosopher who criticized the individualistic emphasis of existentialism and argued for the primacy of the I-Thou relationship (1923). A critic of Zionism, Buber argued for dialogue with Arabs within and outside Israel. Translated the Hebrew Bible with Franz Rosenzweig.

Cohen, Arthur (1928–1986) Jewish theologian. In *The Tremendum* (1981), argued that the Shoah created a caesura, or radical break in history, which could not be bridged by human reason.

Cohen, Hermann (1842–1918) German Jewish philosopher. Founder of the Neo-Kantian movement. Explored a symbiosis of Germanic thought and Jewish thought in his own system. Developed a seminal philosophical reading of Jewish sources in his last work, *Religion of Reason out of the Sources of Judaism* (1919).

cultural-linguistic theory of religion Developed by contemporary Protestant theologian George Lindbeck. Adopting the anthropology of Clifford Geertz and the philosophy of Ludwig Wittgenstein, Lindbeck argues that religions are not expressions of common human religious dispositions but are rule-governed cultural systems. Religions are based on ritualized social and cultural "language-games," which adherents need to learn to "play."

deconstruction A method of criticism that examines the limitations of a specific text in its context, highlighting the inability to make foundational claims. For Jewish postmodernists, the tradition of Jewish textuality reflects a parallel resistance to fundamentalism, as texts are interpreted in polyphonic and destabilizing ways.

Derrida, Jacques (b. 1930) French philosopher, exponent of a theory of meaning that regards writing as central, particularly with its need for future interpretation and its openness to misinterpretation. Has written on his Algerian Jewish childhood (*Circonfession*, 1991), but is generally not explicit about Jewish textuality.

Diotima The fictional female teacher of Socrates in Plato's *Symposium*.

Dreyfus affair Infamous case of the wrongful conviction and imprisonment of a French Jewish army officer on charges of treason in 1894. The trial of Alfred Dreyfus became a focal point for anti-Semitism in France in the 1890s. Dreyfus's conviction was subsequently set aside in 1906, largely due to the publication of information gathered by Emile Zola, which indicated that the evidence against Dreyfus had been fabricated by two senior military officers.

Elohim The biblical Hebrew name usually translated as "God" when YHWH is translated as "Lord." Also used as a common noun meaning (human) "judges."

Emancipation Beginning with the French Revolution, a process by which Jews in Europe obtained full civic equality allowing them to participate in mainstream European culture, usually on condition of their abandoning public signs of Jewish religiosity.

essentialism The modern philosophical claim that what things are is determined by their essences and that the essential nature of a thing is more important and more real than the existent entities one encounters.

ethical monotheism A system of thought that identifies the uniqueness of God with the ethical attributes of God and with correlative moral norms for human action. Originated in the late nineteenth century, especially in the work of Hermann Cohen, as a way of accentuating the specific contribution of Judaism to thought and to the study of religion.

excluded middle In traditional, propositional logic, it was assumed that all rational statements must obey the "law of excluded middle": that any quality predicated of a subject must be either P or *not-P*. Postmodern philosophers note that rational statements about inherently vague entities need not obey this law.

Fackenheim, Emil (b. 1916) German Jewish philosopher, for decades a refugee in Canada (now an Israeli citizen). Explored the religious dimension of German Idealism and the philosophical significance of the Shoah.

foundationalism The effort to identify a single rational foundation for all knowledge: that is, to find the single form of intuition or of reasoning with reference to which we can verify all claims about what we know and what we should do. According to critics of modern philosophy, from Wittgenstein to the postmodernists, modern philosophy's basic mark and error is its foundationalism.

Gemara   In the redaction of the Talmud from the second to the sixth centuries C.E., the portion devoted to the Amoraic rabbis' commentary upon the Mishnah. See Talmud.

Gesetz and *Gebot*   Literally, "law" and "command." In Rosenzweig's work, this opposition contrasts the revealing presence of God in the command with the fixed rule of law.

Gikatilla, Joseph (1248–1325)   Spanish Jewish mystic and philosopher. Author of *Shaarei Orah*. Focused on the power of the Name of God in theurgic practice and theosophical speculation.

grammatology   Literally, "the science of writing." In Derrida's work, including his book by the same name (1967), this is the reorientation of thought to focus on the written text rather than the spoken word. Written text, or scripture, offers distinctive insight into the ways we communicate and understand the world.

grapheme   Literally, "a written thing." The most basic unit of written systems or texts.

Greenberg, Irving (b. 1933)   Theologian in the American Modern Orthodox movement, founder of CLAL, the National Jewish Center for Learning and Leadership, and author of *The Jewish Way* (1988). CLAL fosters pluralism and common understanding among the leaders of all denominations of Judaism *(clal yisrael)*.

Habermas, Jürgen (b. 1929)   German philosopher. Social and political theorist, explored the American pragmatist tradition as resource for refashioning transcendental social theory. Author of *Theory of Communicative Action* (1981).

halakhah   Legal interpretation in rabbinic tradition, literally "the way"; contrasted with aggadah, homiletical interpretation.

Hallel   The psalms of praise (Ps. 113–118) recited for many Jewish festivals.

Hashem   Literally, "the name." Adopted in rabbinic culture as a euphemism for the divine name of God (YHWH) because the name itself was too holy to be uttered.

Hasidism   Eastern European Jewish pietist movement that emerged in the eighteenth century. Some postmodern Jewish theologians have been influenced by Hasidism's emphasis on the more-than-rational dimensions of a life of Torah: myth, mysticism, song, dance, and love.

Haskalah   Enlightenment movement that emerged among Jews in Europe during the nineteenth century, leading to the resurgence of Hebrew language and modern intellectual studies.

Heidegger, Martin (1889–1976)   Phenomenologist and thinker. Explored the relations of language and being. Unrepentant member of the Nazi party. Author of *Being and Time* (1927).

hermeneutics   From the Greek *hermēneuein*, meaning "to understand," "to interpret." In philosophy, *hermeneutics* refers to the art of interpretation, usually the interpretation of texts. As a modern academic discipline, hermeneutics developed from legal interpretation and biblical interpretation in nineteenth-century Germany.

Herzl, Theodor (1860–1904)   Author of *The Jewish State* (1896), founder of political Zionism, galvanized the movement for a secular homeland for the Jews in Palestine.

heteronomous   Literally, "having the law from another." While Kant considers heteronomy immoral, recent thinkers have reconsidered the possibility that another person could be the stimulus and source of the "I" coming to moral responsibility.

Hirsch, Samson Raphael (1808–1888)   Leader of Neo-Orthodoxy, a protest and secessionist movement that arose in protest against Reform Judaism in Germany. Author of *The Nineteen Letters* (1838).

Husserl, Edmund (1859–1938)   Founder of the phenomenological school. Developed a method for exploring the intentionalities of our awareness of things, independent of the question of their objective reality. Asserted that the access to things themselves, to experience in its various structures as present in consciousness, allowed a recovery of experience beyond psychology. Levinas studied with him and translated his work into French.

Immemorial, the   What cannot be remembered, that is, lying beyond the reach of human memory. In contemporary French thought, this refers not to the distant past but to that aspect of the past that consciousness can never account for.

indeterminacy of meaning   In opposition to the theory that each word stands for only one thing, the claim for indeterminacy holds that signs are generally plural and cannot be assigned one specific meaning.

involuntary, the   What cannot be chosen. In contemporary French thought, the way that we are assigned beyond our will to our place in the world. The idea of a people chosen for a relationship with God prior to any choice by that people can be interpreted as an aspect of the involuntary.

Irigaray, Luce (b. 1930) Feminist philosopher and psychoanalyst. A critic of Freudian theory for its masculine-centered concepts, she developed a positive view of women's experiences and bodies.

Jabes, Edmond (1912–1992) Egyptian-born Jewish poet. Explored the way questions work, in an imitation of the Talmud. *The Book of Questions* (1963).

James, William (1842–1910) American philosopher. Responsible for the widespread use of the term *pragmatism*. Psychologist who explored the nature of religious experience and helped determine the direction of both American thought and Husserl's phenomenology.

kabbalah Hebrew word meaning "tradition," referring to the tradition of Jewish mysticism.

kedushah Literally, "sanctification." In general, Judaism requires the actions of human beings to make things holy. *Kedushah* also refers to the specific set of prayers in the daily *Amidah* that proclaim God's holiness.

Kristeva, Julia (b. 1941) French feminist theorist. Her work represents an important synthesis of semiotics and psychoanalytic theory and practice. Author of *Desire in Language* (1980).

Lacan, Jacques (b. 1901) French psychoanalyst and semiotic theorist. Combined Freudian theory with semiotics and with a Heideggerian analysis of human existence and interpretation. Author of *Écrits* (1966).

Lanzmann, Claude (b. 1925) French film director, whose epic documentary *Shoah* was composed of interviews with survivors and perpetrators of the Nazi destruction of European Jewry.

logic of origin In Hermann Cohen's work, especially *The Logic of Pure Cognition* (1914), the principle that knowledge arises from the logical beginnings and not from the givenness of experience or of things. The process of definition produces the reality of what can be known.

logocentrism A philosophic tendency based on the assumption that what is real and important is determined through logic, or more generally, through language. In contemporary usage, the word generally carries negative connotations, as postmodern theorists are suspicious of the idea that things must be rational in order to be.

Lurianic kabbalah A form of Jewish mysticism originating in the sixteenth century, in which the process of creation is interpreted in a richly dialectical manner, as encompassing contraction and suffering.

Lyotard, Jean-François (1924–1998) French philosopher. Expounded the idea of postmodernism as the end of the possibility of a master narrative, a story that encompasses the whole history of ideas in a one-directional sweep. Explores the trope of the Jew in relation to Levinas. Author of *The Differend* (1983) and *The Postmodern Condition* (1979).

Mendelssohn, Moses (1729–1786) German Jewish philosopher. Proponent of Enlightenment in German and French culture, as well as of emancipation for Jews. Inspired the Haskalah.

midrash Literally, "searching out." Refers to Jewish figurative reading of biblical texts. The practice was developed by the rabbinic Sages during the first to the fifth centuries.

Mikra'ot Gedolot Anthology of medieval rabbinic commentaries on the biblical text.

Mishnah The normative anthology of rabbinic legal texts, organized in six orders, promulgated around 220 C.E. by Judah the Patriarch. The Talmuds are commentaries on this anthology.

mitzvot Literally, "commandments." The core of Jewish religion, the mitzvot include requirements about prayer, behavior, social organization, diet, clothing, agriculture, and other aspects of daily life.

monologic Describes the reasoning of a solitary thinker. Contrasts with *dialogic* thought, which depends on the interaction of the thinking self with others.

Neo-Orthodoxy The nineteenth-century German Jewish movement to define traditional Judaism by way of a rational and absolute system of belief. Diverged from more liberal Jewish thought, advancing the claim that the Torah was literally given to Moses at Sinai.

Neoplatonism The school of philosophy and rational mysticism that thrived from late antiquity through the medieval period, drawing on a view of the world as an emanation of the Divine Intellect.

Neo-Scholasticism A restoration of medieval scholastic thought in the service of Catholic resistance to modern science and modern culture, focusing on the works of Thomas Aquinas and emphasizing realism in the theory of knowledge and morals.

Onkelos   Rabbinically authorized version of the Aramaic translation of the Pentateuch, attributed to Onkelos the Proselyte, of the
late first century C.E.

pantextual deconstruction   The claim that only texts exist, and that
they deconstruct themselves—that is, they refuse stable meanings,
making constant recourse to other texts.

Peirce, Charles Sanders (1839–1914)   Philosopher, mathematician
and scientist, founder of the American philosophic method of
pragmatism and the logical method of semiotics. For a general introduction, see R. Corrington, *An Introduction to C. S. Peirce*
(1993); on Peirce's relevance to postmodern Jewish philosophy, see
P. Ochs, *Peirce, Pragmatism, and the Logic of Scripture* (1998).

peshat   In rabbinic Judaism, the plain sense of a scriptural text (literally, the way the meaning is "spread out"): more precisely, the
meaning of a text in its literary context.

phenomenology   A school of twentieth-century philosophy that examines the workings of consciousness in order to understand the
transcendental conditions of our experience, noting the limits of
our minds' power to represent and know reality.

Pirke Avot   Literally, "Chapters of the Fathers." A tractate of the
Mishnah (from the division titled "Damages," *Nezikin*) that con-
tains the collected practical wisdom of the rabbinic Sages.

polyphony   A word with Greek roots, meaning "many voices."
Refers to the quality produced by different voices within one piece,
whether of choral performance or of the different registers in a
written text.

polysemic   A term in contemporary theory of interpretation that
refers to the capacity of a word, text, or sign to mean more than
one thing.

positive revelation   The claim that God revealed concrete instruction, a written text or an oral instruction, and that we still possess
this concrete information from God. A natural revelation would
be universally available, like the laws of nature or ethical principles such as the value of life. A negative revelation would be a
prohibition on knowing God that was somehow revealed, like the
prohibition of idolatry.

pragmatics   In the terminology initiated by philosopher Charles
Morris, this is the subfield of semiotics (sign theory) that examines
the use of signs and the influence or force they exert. Morris contrasted pragmatics with semantics, which examines the relations

between signs and their intended meanings, and with morphemics, which examines the material properties of signs. Today, *pragmatics* is applied more broadly to denote the study of signs as activities in relation to other signs.

psak   A legal judgment in rabbinic Judaism.

Quine, Willard (b. 1908)   Philosophic logician influenced by the pragmatists' theories of truth and meaning. He has helped undermine modernist efforts to insulate theory from linguistic practice, and thence, from direct interactions with the worlds of practical experience.

Rashi [Rabbi Solomon ben Isaac](1040–1105)   Northern French Jewish exegete. His commentaries on both the Scriptures and the Talmud have been the standard guide to Jewish readings for centuries.

reductionism   The tendency to reduce the complex and multilayered structures of reality to one plane of existence.

reify   To treat an abstraction or concept as if it were concrete.

Responsa   Legal response literature in rabbinic Judaism: a rabbi's reply, often by letter, to a legal query.

Rorty, Richard (b. 1929)   Philosopher and literary theorist; advocate of a form of postmodern cultural criticism labeled "neopragmatism." His first well known work was *Philosophy and the Mirror of Nature* (1979). For more recent work, see *Objectivsm, Relativism, and Truth* (1991).

Rosenzweig, Franz (1886–1929)   German Jewish philosopher and theologian. Returned to Jewish practice from an assimilated liberal family. Translated the Bible into German with Buber. Author of *The Star of Redemption* (1921).

Rubenstein, Richard (b. 1924)   American Jewish theologian. In proximity to Protestant "Death of God" theologians, explored the crisis of the Shoah. Author of *After Auschwitz* (1966).

Samuelson, Norbert (b. 1936)   American Jewish philosopher. Founding organizer of Academy for Jewish Philosophy. Analyzes the interaction between modern science and Jewish philosophy. Author of *Judaism and the Doctrine of Creation* (1994).

Schelling, F. W. J. (1775–1854)   German Idealist. His later lectures on mythology and revelation argue that there is a negative, a priori philosophy that grasps the concepts of possible experience, and a positive philosophy that depends on experience, particularly of God and of positive revelation.

Scholasticism A philosophical movement in medieval Judaism and Christianity that combined Platonic and Aristotelian thought with earlier traditions of biblical interpretation. The Jewish proponents of this movement included Saadiah Gaon, Maimonides, Nachmanides, Gersonides; among the Christians were Anselm, Bonaventura, Thomas Aquinas, Duns Scotus, and Ockham.

Sefer Yetsirah Literally, "Book of Creation." An early Jewish mystical text that develops the idea of a set of emanations in God and emphasizes the role of Hebrew letters in creation.

semiological web The idea that signs have meanings not in reference to things outside a web or system of signs, but through interconnections and cross-references within the sign web.

semiotics The study of the behavior of signs (symbols, words, marks), where a sign is something that stands for something else. Charles Peirce founded the American tradition of semiotics, characterized by the doctrine that signs are typically tripartite phenomena: *things* that mean *something* to a particular *interpreter*. Ferdinand de Saussure founded the Continental tradition of semiotics (semiology), characterized by the dual distinction of signs (*signes,* or signifiers) from their objects (*signifiés,* or signifieds).

Shabbat The Sabbath.

Shalom Nekevah A new welcoming ceremony for Jewish girls on their first Shabbat, paralleling the *Shalom Zakhar* ceremony for boys.

Shekhinah In rabbinic Judaism, the female "Divine Presence" in the world.

Shoah Refers to the Holocaust; literally, "destruction, desolation." The Hebrew word is increasingly preferred among Jewish thinkers, since *Holocaust* bears the inappropriate connotation of a burnt offering in the Temple.

Sprachdenken Literally, "speech-thinking." A philosophic practice developed by Rosenzweig and others, as a turn toward thinking not in pure logic but in spoken dialogue. A kind of existential thinking about language in use, this method implies a fundamental critique of all idealist philosophy.

Talmud Literally, "learning." Also refers to the foundational literature of rabbinic Judaism: two voluminous sets of second- through fifth-century commentaries on the Mishnah that were redacted, respectively, in the sixth century (Babylonian Talmud) and the fifth century C.E. (Palestinian Talmud).

talmud torah   Study of Torah, in rabbinic Judaism.

Tanakh   Acronym for the Hebrew Bible, a canon that includes the Torah (the five books of Moses), the *Nevi'im* ("Prophets") and the *Ketuvim* ("Writings").

teshuvah   Repentance, in rabbinic Judaism; the activity of "returning" to God, or of reconciliation with God's will.

tikkun   "Repair"; in rabbinic Judaism, the concept of spiritual repair, as in repairing a broken world *(tikkun olam)*. In Lurianic kabbalah, the concept of repairing God's shattered Other.

Torah   Hebrew word with several levels of meaning: (1) used as a common noun, it means "teaching" or "instruction" in general; (2) used as a proper noun, in its narrowest sense it refers to the "Ten Words" that God gave Moses and the people of Israel on Mount Sinai, or more broadly, to the entire "Five Books of Moses," or Pentateuch, which provides the scriptural context for teaching God's written word; or most broadly, all aspects of God's word to Israel. The Rabbinic Sages interpreted the word even more broadly to include (3) all teaching, discussion, and interpretation that extended the meanings of God's written word in new and differing contexts. Furthermore, rabbinic doctrine holds that two Torahs were revealed on Mount Sinai: an explicitly written Torah *(torah she b'khtav)*, preserved as the Hebrew Bible; and the oral Torah *"torah she b'al peh,"* which discloses the meaning of the written Torah for a given historical community (see Mishnah, *Pirke Avot* ["Chapters of the Fathers"] 1:1).

totalism   A thought process that subsumes every particular thing or action under a single concept. To totalize is to refuse the existence of an outside or of an other to this single, overarching concept.

totalizing master narratives   Philosophical interpretations in which all individual texts or stories are assigned a particular place or role in the thought system of a main (master) story.

tsedakah   In rabbinic Judaism, the virtue of charity (literally, "righteousness"); refers to the justice of providing for those in need.

tsimtsum   Contraction, limitation: In the kabbalah attributed to Isaac Luria, this is the doctrine that God contracted the divine self to make "room" for creation—hence the doctrines of divine and of pious self-limitation.

Vico, Giambattista (1668–1744)   Italian philosopher. Devised the idea of social sciences as a counterpoint to Descartes's physical sciences. Claimed that the history of institutions was the history of human consciousness.

Zohar A Jewish mystical text written in the thirteenth century by Moses de León. An extended commentary on the Torah, the Zohar is the seminal text of Jewish mysticism from the middle ages to the present. The depth of its theological and spiritual exegesis is a source for the multiple layers and ranges of meaning explored in postmodern Jewish thought.

About the Contributors

Almut Sh. Bruckstein teaches Jewish philosophy at the Hebrew University, the Rothberg School for overseas students. She has written significant publications on Maimonides, Hermann Cohen, Franz Rosenzweig, and Emmanuel Levinas. She is currently working on a translation and commentary on Cohen's interpretation of Maimonides.

Robert Gibbs teaches philosophy at the University of Toronto. He is the author of *Correlations in Rosenzweig and Levinas,* and most recently of *Why Ethics: Signs of Responsibilities.* His work addresses Jewish philosophy in the tradition of Hermann Cohen, Franz Rosenzweig, Martin Buber, and Emmanuel Levinas and engages both contemporary Continental thought and American pragmatism.

Yudit Kornberg Greenberg is professor of religious studies at Rollins College, Winter Park, Florida. She writes on issues related to language, love, and the body in religious and philosophical writings. Her most recent publication is *Better Than Wine: Love, Poetry, and Prayer in the Thought of Franz Rosenzweig,* and she is currently completing a manuscript entitled *The Kisses of His Mouth: Divine Love and Eros in Jewish Thought.*

Steven Kepnes is associate professor of philosophy and religion and director of Jewish Studies at Colgate University. He was a visiting scholar at the Hebrew University and at the Shalom Hartman Institute for Advanced Jewish Studies from 1993 to 1995. He is author of *Interpreting Judaism in a Postmodern Age*; *The Text as Thou: Martin Buber's Dialogical Hermeneutics and Narrative Theology* and coeditor, with David Tracy, of *The Challenge of Psychology to Faith.* His articles on Jewish thought have appeared in such journals as the *Journal of Jewish Studies, Soundings,* and the *Harvard Theological Review.* He is also Judaism editor for *Religious Studies Review.*

Peter Ochs is the Edgar Bronfman Professor of Modern Judaic Studies at the University of Virginia, and co-founder of the Societies for Textual Reasoning, and for Scriptural Reasoning. He is the author of *Peirce, Pragmatism, and the Logic of Scripture,* and coauthor of *Reviewing the Covenant: Eugene Borowitz and the Postmodern Renewal of Theology.* He is the author or editor of a number of works on the relations between rabbinic and American varieties of pragmatism and semiotics, and between Jewish and Christian theologies.

Susan E. Shapiro teaches modern Jewish thought and philosophy of religion in the Department of Religion at Columbia University and recently has been visiting professor in the Program on Women and Religion at the Harvard University Divinity School. Her research engages a range of issues, represented by the following selection of her writing: "A Matter of Discipline: Reading for Gender in Jewish Philosophy"; "Failing Speech: Post-Holocaust Writing and the Discourse of Postmodernism"; and "The Uncanny Jew: A Brief History of the Image."

Elliot R. Wolfson is Abraham Lieberman Professor of Hebrew and Judaic Studies and director of religious studies at the New York University. He is the author of several books and many essays on the history of Jewish mysticism, with a particular emphasis on hermeneutics and gender studies. His *Through a Speculum That Shines: Vision and Imagination in Medieval Jewish Mysticism* (1994) was awarded the American Academy of Religion Award for Excellence in Historical Studies (1995) and the National Jewish Book Award for Outstanding Scholarship (1995).

Edith Wyschogrod is the J. Newton Rayzor Professor of Philosophy and Religious Thought at Rice University. She is a past president of the American Academy of Religion. Her most recent books are *An Ethics of Remembering: History, Heterology, and the Nameless Others* and *Saints and Postmodernism: Revisioning Moral Philosophy.*

Index